GO TEAM!

TAKE YOUR TEAM TO THE NEXT LEVEL

Ken Blanchard

Alan Randolph

Peter Grazier

BK

BERRETT-KOEHLER PUBLISHERS, INC.
San Francisco

Berrett-Koehler Publishers, Inc.
235 Montgomery Street, Suite 650
San Francisco, CA 94104-2916
Tel: (415) 288-0260   Fax: (415) 362-2512   www.bkconnection.com

Ordering Information

Quantity sales. Special discounts are available on quantity purchases by corporations, associations,
and others. For details, contact the "Special Sales Department" at the Berrett-Koehler address above.

Individual sales. Berrett-Koehler publications are available through most bookstores. They can
also be ordered directly from Berrett-Koehler: Tel: (800) 929-2929; Fax: (802) 864-7626;
www.bkconnection.com

Orders for college textbook/course adoption use. Please contact Berrett-Koehler:
Tel: (800) 929-2929; Fax: (802) 864-7626.

Orders by U.S. trade bookstores and wholesalers. Please contact Publishers Group West,
1700 Fourth Street, Berkeley, CA 94710. Tel: (510) 528-1444; Fax (510) 528-3444.

Berrett-Koehler and the BK logo are registered trademarks of Berrett-Koehler Publishers, Inc.

Printed in the United States of America

Berrett-Koehler books are printed on long-lasting acid-free paper. When it is available, we choose
paper that has been manufactured by environmentally responsible processes. These may include
using trees grown in sustainable forests, incorporating recycled paper, minimizing chlorine in
bleaching, or recycling the energy produced at the paper mill.

Library of Congress Cataloging-in-Publication Data
Blanchard, Kenneth H.
    Go team! : take your team to the next level / by Ken Blanchard, Alan Randolph
  and Peter Grazier.
      p.   cm.
  Includes index.
  ISBN 13:978-1-57675-262-3
    1. Teams in the workplace. I. Randolph, W. Alan. II. Grazier, Peter, 1946-
  III. Title.
  HD66.B548   2005
  658.4'022—dc22   2004062786

FIRST EDITION
10 09 08 07 06 05   10 9 8 7 6 5 4 3 2 1

Copyediting and proofreading by PeopleSpeak.
Book design and composition by Beverly Butterfield, Girl of the West Productions.
Indexing by Rachel Rice.

Dedicated to the memory of
John P. Carlos,
the Great Storyteller

CONTENTS

FOREWORD

We were honored when Ken, Alan, and Peter asked us to write the foreword to their new book, *Go Team!* Ken and Alan have been our friends and colleagues for more than thirty years. We are delighted that they are adding this guide to understanding and achieving "Next Level" team status to the Blanchard library on team excellence.

For the past two decades significant changes have been occurring in our workplaces involving how work is structured and how decisions are made. Organizations have had to reinvent themselves to meet the demands of a rapidly changing global environment. Productivity, quality, and human satisfaction have increased in those organizations that have begun to use high involvement management practices. And teams have been the cornerstones of many of these successful change efforts.

Teamwork and collaboration are how work gets done effectively. Team-based practices, when successfully implemented, lead to higher productivity, increased satisfaction, and better employee health, and they promote our democratic values. Most people today participate in at least one and sometimes many different teams. Unfortunately, those teams often do not perform up to their potential. One of the major barriers to effectively implementing teams is that people have not been properly trained to function in teams as contributing team members.

When we wrote, with Ken Blanchard, *The One Minute Manager Builds High Performing Teams* in 1989, we were interested in providing a basic understanding of

- The characteristics of high performing teams
- The stages of team development
- The leadership behaviors appropriate at each stage

That book, now in its second edition, has become a best-selling standard for understanding the core essentials for building high performing teams, and thousands of people have participated in training programs based on those concepts. The popular sequel, *High Five! The Magic of Working Together*, written with Sheldon Bowles, builds on those concepts and through an engaging parable shows what individuals and organizations must do to build successful teams.

Go Team! Take Your Team to the Next Level expands on the principles in these two books by building on ideas in the bestselling book by Ken, Alan, and John Carlos: *The Three Keys to Empowerment*. Now, Ken, Alan, and Peter have created a wonderful field guide that provides practical ideas and activities for moving teams to the Next Level. As you read this book, you will gain both the ability and the confidence to make effective use of *information-sharing skills* to build trust and responsibility, clear *boundary-setting skills* to create freedom, and *self-managing skills* to get great results.

This field guide will serve many teams for many years as an outstanding resource to use to increase team skills, productivity, and morale. It is an ideal follow-up to training in basic team concepts and can help ensure application and sustainability in real-world team settings.

Excellence in leadership, innovation, quality, service, productivity, and human satisfaction in the twenty-first century will best come from people working in teams that can use their potential, knowledge, and motivation. *Go Team!* is a tool that can help make that happen, and we hope you will use it to *Take Your Team to the Next Level.*

Don Carew
Eunice Parisi-Carew
Founding Associates of the Ken Blanchard Companies
Coauthors of *The One Minute Manager Builds High Performing Teams* and *High Five! The Magic of Working Together*

INTRODUCTION
MOVING TEAMWORK TO THE NEXT LEVEL

People in organizations today are increasingly being called upon to work in teams. This is because the work of organizations has become amazingly complex and changes occur constantly. More and more, companies around the world are using teams to deal with this dynamic world of work.

Unfortunately, too few people really understand how to build a team that puts into action the knowledge, experience, and motivation of its people. We do not have to look very far to see numerous examples of failed team efforts—be they in sports, business, or government. Therefore, it is no surprise that people often give up on the idea of teams and try to go it alone. We do not believe that is an effective solution for today's workplace. *Go Team!* is our game plan for building better teams—Next Level Teams.

What are Next Level Teams, and what benefits do they bring to the table? First, the benefits: Next Level Teams

- Use all team members' ideas and motivation

- Make better use of the team members' and team leader's time

- Increase productivity and satisfaction for you, your team, and the organization

Second, what are Next Level Teams? They are teams that can

- Use *information sharing* to build high levels of trust and responsibility
- Use *clear boundaries* to create the freedom to act responsibly
- Use *self-managing skills* to make team decisions and get great results

Once the picture of a Next Level Team is clear, you and your team members can assess how you operate now. Then you can begin the process of becoming a Next Level Team that gets great results.

Those of you who are fans of Ken Blanchard books will notice that *Go Team!* is a departure from Ken's easy-reading business parables. This book is intended to be a working guide filled with detailed instructions for people who want to build high performing teams.

Go Team! will take you through *three steps to great results:*

Step 1   Begin learning Next Level skills
Step 2   Accelerate the change
Step 3   Master the skills

Each step is designed to guide your team to the Next Level. As you, your team members, and your leader move through the book together, responsibility will shift naturally from your leader to your team. You will learn how to use your ideas more effectively, make excellent team decisions, and feel the pride of having contributed in new and more meaningful ways.

Your leader will also appreciate your team's move to the Next Level because he or she will have new opportunities to help the team. What leader hasn't been frustrated by a lack of time to plan work, think ahead, receive training, coach team members, or investigate new equipment that may be needed in the future?

As your group moves to become a Next Level Team, you will enhance creativity, increase satisfaction, develop a sense of group pride, and achieve outstanding results. You will suddenly find your team soaring above the ordinary.

Learn what Next Level Teams are and what they can do. Then use this book as a resource and take three steps with your team to get great results. Enjoy the journey—and get ready to soar!

ONE

Understanding Next Level Teams

a picture of your future

You've no doubt heard about teamwork and its importance in today's workplace. Perhaps your organization has even tried to do more with teams and has preached teamwork.

But most people are much more familiar with the idea of a work group. It's the front line of an organization where the product is made or the service is provided. The idea of work groups is based on a view of work that is rooted in the old notion of an organization with rigid lines of managerial control, authority, and responsibility. In other words, those in leadership positions tend to assume they should make most decisions about the work, and employees tend to assume they should do what they are told by the leaders.

WHY IS A NEW KIND OF TEAM NEEDED TODAY?

In today's rapidly changing business environment, concentrating decision-making authority with a few people no longer gets the kind of results that are needed. Additionally, centralized decision making places an undue burden on those making the decisions and is frustrating to those who cannot act until the decisions are made. Communication in the traditional work system simply moves too slowly. Because decision making is slow, people are inhibited from taking action in a timely and responsible fashion.

With this approach to work, organizations cannot compete successfully, and people throughout the company feel they are not valued. The result is low motivation and low company performance. Moving key decisions closer to the front line makes good business sense. This approach is at the core of teamwork that gets great results. But it means operating in a new world for most people.

WHAT KIND OF TEAM GETS GREAT RESULTS?

To succeed in today's complex and changing business environment, we must learn a new way of working in teams. We must take our teams to the Next Level. This means creating teams that release the power of team members—power that comes from their knowledge, experience, and internal motivation.

For example, a supervisor we know was frustrated by the amount of time he spent performing tasks that, although important from an administrative viewpoint, did not seem to maximize the use of his talents and skills in the organization. He wondered how he might change this. He thought about the valuable time he spent approving small purchases of tools and supplies for his group. Then he considered how he could better use the abilities of his people in performing tasks that did not make the best use of his experience and skills.

One of these tasks was ordering small tools and materials for the team each time a team member came to him with a request. So he taught the team members how to place the orders themselves and began delegating these purchases to the team.

He allowed them to submit small orders directly without his approval. Initially, he placed a boundary on the purchases—a cost limit of $100—but he later widened the *boundary* as the team's (and his) comfort level grew. Team members had the authority to order needed supplies more easily without the delay of the supervisor's approval. His team members felt great. The cost of supplies decreased by 20 percent as people took more care in ordering only those materials that were really needed.

Sounds easy, doesn't it? But, given our history and comfort with traditional work groups, we have a lot to unlearn to take steps like this supervisor did. And, while people may complain about managerial control, they take comfort in not having to take too much responsibility for decisions and outcomes. Yet taking that responsibility is exactly what is required to move teams to new levels of excitement, energy, and performance.

What Is a Next Level Team?

Taking your team to the Next Level builds a team that

1. *Is a highly skilled, interactive group of people that uses the ideas and motivation of all team members*
2. *Uses information sharing to build high levels of trust and responsibility*
3. *Uses clear boundaries to create the freedom and responsibility to accomplish tasks in an efficient manner*
4. *Makes effective use of the time and talents of team members and their team leader*
5. *Uses self-managing skills to make team decisions and generate great results for the team, its members, and the organization.*

Next Level Teamwork in action

The manager of a newly developed performance improvement department at a nuclear power plant was asked to assume responsibility for the site's newsletter. Along with the newsletter came its editor, Bill, as a new member of the manager's team. During Bill's first meeting with the manager, he complained that management had restricted him to writing a four-page monthly newsletter for a construction project of six thousand workers. Bill felt strongly that expanding the newsletter to six or eight pages would greatly improve it.

The manager wondered quietly how much additional work Bill could really do. After all, he would be responsible for collecting the information, writing the articles, taking pictures, working with the printer, and mailing the newsletter to the entire workforce. The manager was tempted to give Bill a number (he felt ten pages would be the limit) but instead gave him a clear performance objective. He said, "Bill, write whatever has to be written to adequately communicate to the people on this project, and if it gets too big, I'll tell you."

Bill left the office with new energy and enthusiasm and began to work on improving the newsletter. Using his ingenuity, he solicited help from others on his team and on the project: the graphic artist, the site photographer, the activities coordinator, craftsmen in the field, and others. Within ten months, they had transformed the newsletter into a thirty-two-page magazine and the most respected communication tool on the project. It was so informative and gained so much respect that the project's owner, the electric utility, began requesting eighty-eight copies each month for its board of directors.

As a member of the manager's team, Bill was given full responsibility for the effectiveness of the site's newsletter. In turn, Bill solicited the help of his fellow team members. As they gained comfort with their newfound responsibility and authority, they began to experiment more and more, improving the newsletter significantly and ultimately creating the site's most important communication tool.

In this case, delegating complete ownership and responsibility to Bill and the other team members created a great newsletter and a great result.

QUESTIONS TO CONSIDER

Taking your team to the Next Level

In the above example, we explained how Bill and the other team members were given expanded responsibility and authority to make decisions about the newsletter. For example, they

- Decided how many pages the newsletter should contain
- Decided the content of the newsletter
- Were responsible for controlling the newsletter's budget
- Could bring in others to help with articles and pictures
- Answered all inquiries regarding the newsletter
- Decided how many hours they should work to achieve the desired results

Thinking about this example, how could you and your team members make good use of expanded authority and more direct ownership of your tasks? What decisions does your supervisor make now that could be made by your team?

NEXT LEVEL TEAMS AND THE LEADER'S ROLE

Historically, decisions for day-to-day work and overall responsibility for the success of a work group have rested with the leader. This was one of the clear expectations of the leader's role. Leaders became comfortable with this responsibility, in fact, placing high value on this exercise of power.

Additionally, through most of the last century, certain management theories taught that workers would not accept responsibility and, in fact, would abuse time if left unsupervised. As a result, leaders were expected to closely supervise their people and certainly not delegate responsibility for work decisions.

So when we talk about shifting decisions closer to the point of action and putting them in the hands of the team, this contradicts the traditional role of the leader. One of the primary questions of managers, supervisors, and team leaders is, "What will my role be in this new environment? If my team takes on more of the day-to-day work decisions, what will I do?"

In point of fact, delegating daily task decisions actually enhances the role of the leader, as well as the role of the team members. The leader can take on new tasks, particularly those that seem to get sidelined in favor of the more immediate daily decisions. One manager explained her appreciation for Next Level Teams by stating, "Delegating certain day-to-day decisions and tasks to the team has allowed me to concentrate on issues of strategic importance to our department." Too much of her time had been spent fighting fires. Now, with the team's ability to fight the fires, she tackled new tasks with greater potential to add value.

To understand the positive impact a Next Level Team has on its leader, consider what a team leader might be able to do if he or she had an extra two hours in the workday to spend on other activities. Indeed, we have asked this question to many leaders, and some of the responses we hear include

- Spend more time planning the work
- Look ahead to contemplate new equipment that may be needed
- Address some of the issues that impede the team's work
- Spend more time coaching and counseling team members
- Attend a work-related conference
- Interact more with customers
- Take a training course and learn new skills

It is important to understand that the shift to a Next Level Team has the additional benefit of freeing up the team leader, supervisor, or manager to focus on how better to serve the team and the organization.

QUESTIONS TO CONSIDER

Your leader's role in Next Level Teamwork

If your manager, supervisor, or team leader had an extra two hours each day—gained by expanding the responsibility and authority of your team—what new activities could he or she engage in that would add more value to the group, department, or organization?

BENEFITS OF NEXT LEVEL TEAMS

We have explored how Next Level Teams could impact your day-to-day actions in the workplace. We have also considered how the roles of leaders and team members change in such an environment. These are significant and powerful changes in how an organization operates. But is this change justified? Is it worth the effort? Does it really get great results? Let's look at two more examples.

 EXAMPLES

The convenience store chain

A convenience store chain on the West Coast was experiencing employee turnover rates of 140 to 220 percent per year, normal for this industry. When the company implemented Next Level Team concepts, the turnover rate dropped to 70 percent. The considerable savings in recruiting time and expenses, training of new personnel, and disruptions to operations were certainly worth the effort from the company's perspective.

Employees also benefited from the change. Today, exit interviews indicate that when people decide to leave the company to take on new job opportunities, they are not leaving because they are unhappy. A typical response from team members before moving to the Next Level was "I was told to sell my soul for a minimum-wage job." Today a typical response is "I had probably the best first job experience I could imagine. I plan to be a customer of theirs for a long time to come." Next Level Teams in this company have created a more satisfied and loyal workforce, and the benefits for the company have been outstanding.

The telecommunications company

A telecommunications company on the East Coast made the move to Next Level Teams. Once in place, these teams were allowed to assess production methods and then make and implement suggestions for improvement. As you might expect, the teams started slowly with very few suggestions, but their suggestions did have a positive impact. Within two years, the number of suggestions had grown to more than five per employee per year, which far exceeds the national average of less than one suggestion per employee per year. Furthermore, the number of ideas implemented increased quickly to exceed 60 percent of the ideas suggested—a figure nearly six times the national average for suggestions implemented. The suggestions that were implemented saved the company hundreds of thousands of dollars. Equally important was the change in attitude of the team members. One team member said, "It doesn't matter what name is on the plaque outside; the company belongs to me and my team as much as it belongs to anyone."

QUESTIONS TO CONSIDER

The benefits of your team moving to the Next Level

Using the two examples above to stimulate your thinking, what do you see as potential benefits of your team moving to the Next Level? How would your work as a Next Level Team benefit the company or your department? How would it benefit your team leader? And finally, how might it benefit you and your team members?

PICTURING YOUR WORK GROUP
AS A NEXT LEVEL TEAM

You have now begun to understand what a Next Level Team is and why it is so important in today's business climate. Simply put, the world of work has become too complex and dynamic for individuals to go it alone or for traditional work groups, operating with limited authority, to be successful. You and your organization need Next Level Teams that have expanded authority to act, release the creative energies of people, and provide opportunities for your team to add greater value to the organization.

Next Level Teams encourage everyone to feel valued, responsible, and engaged in the work. All participants can take pride in using their knowledge, experience, and motivation to achieve great results that will benefit the team and the organization.

As you prepare for the journey of creating your own Next Level Team, take a moment to think about what we have discussed thus far. You have probably gained some insights into your own team, and perhaps a few questions have popped into your mind. At this point it would be helpful for you to consider your team as it is today and how it compares to a Next Level Team. We encourage you to take a few minutes to discuss the following questions with your team.

MOVING FROM AN IDEA INTO ACTION

While the idea of molding your group into a Next Level Team may be appealing, it is important to recognize that understanding the idea and actually doing it are two different things. Moving your team to the Next Level, while challenging, is cer-

Your team now

How do Next Level Teams differ from the way your team currently operates? For example, as of today,

- *Does everyone on your team feel engaged, valued, and proud as a member of the team?*
- *Does your team have and accept the authority to make decisions about its tasks?*
- *Do you understand the boundaries of your team's authority and could this authority be expanded?*
- *Does your team know how to manage itself to get work done?*
- *Does your team achieve truly great results?*

tainly doable and worth the effort. Next Level Teams can deal with complexity and change in truly amazing ways. They can also make you feel more engaged and valued at work.

The remainder of this book will take you through the following three steps to get your team to the Next Level:

During this exciting journey, you will learn to use the three key skills of a Next Level Team:

Three Steps to Next Level Teamwork

STEP ONE
Begin learning Next Level skills

STEP TWO
Accelerate the change

STEP THREE
Master the skills

- Use *information sharing* to build high levels of trust and responsibility
- Use *clear boundaries* to create the freedom to act responsibly
- Use *self-managing skills* to make decisions and get great results

Next Level Teams are empowered to excel, while traditional work groups are disabled. When you put fences around people, you get sheep.

Next Level Teamwork replaces self-interest, dependency, and control with partnership, responsibility, and commitment.

This journey will change you and your team members and the way you work together. At times it may be challenging, but with this book as a guide, your journey will be easier. And in a relatively short period of time you will be at the Next Level, wondering why you did not do this before.

Begin Learning Next Level Skills

TWO

Use Information to Build Responsibility

How do you move your team to the Next Level? The change begins as you learn and apply Next Level skills. This chapter will get your team started as you learn how to use information to build responsibility.

DECISIONS REQUIRE INFORMATION

In any process of change, there has to be a starting point. Let's pretend that you are an architect and have been asked to design a house for a family. You need to know a few things first before you can develop a concept of what the house should look like. But let's also pretend that you have been told you cannot speak with the family about their wants and needs. You must design the house based on your own assumptions.

Puzzled, you proceed to design a house for the "average" family of four, located in a moderate climate. When you finally meet the family, you learn that there are seven children and that the house will be located in a coastal village in Iceland. Needless to say, you are surprised. You are also disappointed because you will need to do the work over again. You did your best but still wasted valuable time and energy, and the house you designed does not work for the family.

Under normal circumstances, you would have asked questions at the beginning of the project, such as,

- How large is the family?
- How many children are there and what are their ages?
- Does an elderly parent or someone else also live with the family?
- Where will the house be located and what is the climate like there?
- What style of home is wanted?
- Does the family have any special needs?
- Is the house to be in a town or in the country?

Of course a house would never be designed without first gathering all the relevant information and giving it to the architect. The point of this example is to emphasize the *importance of information in making good decisions.*

How does this relate to your team and your organization? Let's look at a real-world situation.

 EXAMPLES

Next level teamwork in action

The management team on a construction project decided to begin sharing information with the crews about productivity rates for various aspects of the work. These rates were used to estimate the cost of the project and develop a budget for the work. In the past, these rates had been closely guarded. They had never before been shared with the craftsmen who would perform the work.

•

When the labor rates for installing reinforcing steel were shared with the ironworkers, they were curious to see if they could beat the budgeted rate. By the time they finished the work, they had cut 25 percent off the allocated hours per ton and saved the contractor a considerable amount of money.

Whether we are operating from an executive suite or pushing a broom on the third shift, when we make decisions, we need information. Operating as a Next Level Team steps up the level of information sharing because team members play a larger role in monitoring their own work. People simply need better information to make better decisions. As information is shared freely, more brainpower is enlisted for problem solving and business growth.

 EXAMPLES

Examples of Next Level information sharing

Frontline production workers at Chesebrough Ponds, Inc., routinely scan online inventory reports from the company's distribution centers and make adjustments to their production schedules.

Workers at a small Xerox production facility generated over $3 million in savings per year when given information about competitors' costs.

Dynamically growing Whole Foods Market, Inc., makes salary information on every person—including executives—available to all team members.

As business changes, the nature of work needs to change. Relationships, responsibilities, and information flow between management and the workforce must change to meet the demand for ever-improving performance. The move to Next Level

Teams begins with sharing the information necessary for people to carry out their work effectively and efficiently. Information sharing is absolutely essential for solving the problems that plague organizations.

 EXAMPLES

Information sharing and problem solving

In training sessions for Next Level Teams, an exercise called the "Polygon Puzzle" is used to demonstrate the power of information sharing. Participants are asked to assemble a large puzzle composed of colored plastic pieces. The puzzle is difficult to assemble, so each participant is given a card with a clue to the solution. For five minutes, participants share the clues verbally with those at their table. For another five minutes, they share the clues with all participants. This encourages verbal communication, listening, and sharing of information.

Finally, all of the participants, working as a large team, are given five more minutes to assemble the puzzle. As difficult as the puzzle is, it is almost always assembled within the time allowed if the clues are shared properly.

The rich discussion following the exercise brings out important points about how critical information is for problem solving and how every team member has information that can be vital in solving the problem. It also reveals the barriers to information sharing that hold teams back from achieving effective solutions.

Assessing information sharing in your team

*Using the above examples about information sharing to stimu-
late your thinking, how would you assess the level of information
sharing in your team? Is your team given information that will
help you make better decisions about the work? Do your team
members openly share work-related information with each other?
Do they share it with management?*

WHAT INFORMATION TO SHARE?

The following story illustrates how team members with information can solve problems that often baffle the experts.

EXAMPLES

The country club

*An exclusive country club had a problem with members taking
home the expensive shampoo from its showers. The club's president had considered all sorts of options to fix the problem but
couldn't find a solution that would not offend the members. Finally, he shared this information with the locker-room attendant,
who responded, "Don't worry, they won't do it anymore." The president looked dumbfounded. The attendant continued, "It's simple,
I'll just take the tops off the shampoo. No one will want to take
the shampoo without the top."*

The sharing of information requires us to change our prior beliefs about what people need to know. If team members are being asked to accept more responsibility and accountability for work performance, then they must be given more resources to affect that performance.

Historically, information has been guarded and held closely at various levels of the organization, each level assuming that to share that information would be to compromise it. Information has been regarded as power, and those holding the information have been seen as more powerful.

But as the examples above suggest, power actually increases as more people are included in the organization's thinking processes. The ironworkers increased production once they had a benchmark, and the locker-room attendant devised a solution once he was aware of the problem.

Information sharing in the workplace is simply the process of communication between people who have mutually held goals. In other words, people who are working toward the same result have a need to help each other by pulling together the best information available.

In the past, the communication was between the team and its team leader or supervisor. In a Next Level Team environ-

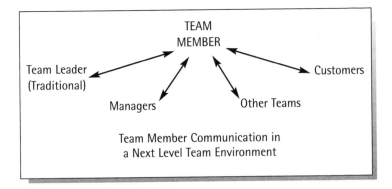

TEAM
MEMBER

Team Leader
(Traditional)

Managers

Other Teams

Customers

Team Member Communication in
a Next Level Team Environment

ment, communication widens to include other work teams, managers, and customers.

In the past, information that was shared with frontline employees was generally only that which was necessary to perform the work. Frontline employees were not asked to make decisions and thus did not need as much information. Next Level Teams are called upon to make and implement decisions, so they need more and different kinds of information.

In a Next Level Team environment, this includes having information such as

- Production rates and quality statistics, both expected and experienced
- Customer feedback, both good and bad
- How well competitors are doing
- How well the organization is doing financially
- Specific problems the organization is having
- Feedback on the team's overall performance
- The health of the industry

Next Level Team members also receive information that needs to be shared to aid in better decisions, such as

- What's working well for the team and what's not
- Ideas for improving work processes to enhance productivity
- Suggestions for better working conditions that yield better results
- Ideas for improving quality
- Suggestions for needed training

Information opens the way to an improved production process

A crew of workers in an auto parts plant spent their time punching out parts on an eight-hundred-ton press. When they needed to change the die on the huge machine for a new run of parts, the machine went off-line, producing no parts and no revenue for the company. Even with their best efforts, the average changeover time was two and one-half hours.

One day a manager mentioned that workers in other countries were changing the same size presses in as little as ten minutes. At first the crew didn't believe him. It just didn't seem humanly possible.

However, after confirming the information, the crew set out to learn more about how to reduce their changeover time. They worked continually on the problem, analyzing and brainstorming new techniques. Some of the crew members were skeptical, stating that they did not believe the changeover could take less than an hour; however, little by little, they chipped away at the time.

Within a year of starting their project, their changeover time dropped to five minutes! Because of the significant time saving, they increased production from their machine by eight hundred hours per year and revenues to the company by $4 million—all because the people on the press team were given new information they could act upon. In this example, great information produced a great result.

Information to be shared

Drawing from the above examples about information sharing, can you think of information that you could share with your team members that might help the team operate better? Is there information that you would like to receive that would help you do a better job? Have you thought about an idea that might improve either the work environment or one of your work processes?

TRUST

Whenever we share information with someone, we create an implied agreement of trust. We trust that the person will handle the information responsibly.

Additionally, when we share information—particularly information of a sensitive nature—a powerful message is sent to the recipient. This unspoken message says that we value the person and trust him or her to act responsibly.

Conversely, when we refuse to share sensitive information with someone, we may send the opposite message: that the person cannot be trusted. This severely hampers the working relationship and, ultimately, opportunities for work improvement.

Next Level Teams become powerful because information is shared openly in an atmosphere of trust and respect. Team members know that they are protected by the bond of trust that exists among them, so they feel freer to offer information that may be sensitive but important to the team's success.

Sharing information enhances trust and the building of productive relationships.

•

THE NEED TO CHANGE OUR
BELIEFS ABOUT INFORMATION

The beliefs we have all acquired about work are deeply embedded in our thinking. These beliefs ultimately become strong drivers of our behavior at work. In the traditional system, we learned that information about an organization and its systems was held tightly at its various levels and parceled out on a need-to-know basis.

The Next Level Team environment turns the old thinking upside-down. Information about the organization and its systems is shared openly so that it can flow naturally to the areas where it is needed most.

Sometimes an organization's sensitive information must be held closely. But much of what has been controlled in the past is information that can and should be shared with everyone. Financial information about the health of the organization, for example, is rarely discussed, although most of this information can be readily found in the organization's annual report to stockholders.

Breaking down this information by business unit, department, or work group becomes meaningful to team members when they can connect how their daily activity contributes to these results and then act in new ways to initiate improvement.

As you share this information, you will unleash a process that will build trust. Ultimately, you will create stronger and more productive working relationships and better performance by your team.

•

There is no joy in possession without sharing.

ERASMO DE ROTTERDAM

•

THREE

Clarify Boundaries to Create Focused Action

When we begin to operate as a Next Level Team, the freedom associated with new responsibilities and authority may seem unclear. What can we do and what can't we do? This is where boundaries become valuable because they help us define our authority clearly and thus allow us to make good decisions and take independent actions.

WHAT IS A BOUNDARY?

A *boundary* is a limit or dividing line. It is a border that defines a territory. For example, the line that divides our property from that of our neighbor's is a boundary, and we know not to cross it when planting trees and shrubs. Because this boundary is clearly defined, we can make decisions on our property without fear of "overstepping our bounds."

When a boundary is not clearly defined, people must attempt to decide for themselves where it is, and history is full of examples of how people have struggled over unclear boundaries.

Independent actions need boundaries so that people can take them with a sense of direction and autonomy and without fear of reprisal. The intent of boundaries in a Next Level Team environment is not to restrict action but rather to create the responsibility and freedom to act. The old system narrows the boundaries, whereas the Next Level approach is to widen them.

In Chapter 1 we spoke of a supervisor who moved his team to the Next Level and allowed team members to make work-related purchases without his involvement. He further defined this new authority by giving them a spending limit of $100, which later increased as everyone grew more comfortable with the new authority.

In this example, the boundary was defined by an action (making a purchase without the supervisor's approval) and a guideline (the $100 spending limit). The new freedom to make a purchase removed the constraint imposed by the previously cumbersome approval process, and the $100 spending limit helped people understand their authority in this new process.

In a traditional culture, one's role is to perform a task. In a Next Level Team environment, one's role is to own an outcome and, therefore, to take actions necessary to achieve that outcome.

Especially at the outset of the change to Next Level Teams, people need clear direction so they can act with freedom and responsibility. They are being asked to take on greater responsibility for the organization's success, but in most cases it will not be clear what that means. Just as people need specific instructions when starting a new job, they will also need clear guidelines for making decisions when operating at the Next Level.

BOUNDARIES CLARIFY ROLES

Historically, people have gone to work to perform tasks. Basically, people were asked to do what they were told. Over the last twenty-five years, however, the "tasks" people are asked to do have evolved significantly. With the introduction of the workplace participation trend, workers have been asked to become more directly involved in process improvement.

Next Level Teams move this involvement to another level by shifting more authority and responsibility for decisions to the front lines. To date, the impact of this change has not been fully appreciated. Consequently, organizations that make the move to Next Level Teams sometimes experience setbacks as they attempt to move forward. All too often, managers think people will just automatically take on focused responsibility, but such a shift demands new insights for both employees and managers. Helping people clearly understand their roles in this environment is critical to success. How should a manager or supervisor act in working with Next Level Teams? How should workers act? When should a worker make a decision, and when should that decision be referred to a higher authority? These are some of the questions encountered as the journey to Next Level Teams begins.

People need answers, and boundaries play a significant part in the process because they help to define tasks, behaviors, and roles. They are critical in providing answers to such questions.

★ **EXAMPLES**

Boundaries provide clear direction

In one financial services organization, the executives and a group of middle managers defined their initial expectations by listing specific tasks that the organization's work groups should be able to perform as they moved to become Next Level Teams. The intent was to create a vision of what their work teams would look like in the future. To develop this list, they discussed the question, "What

·

specifically do you want your work teams doing in the future that they are not doing now?" Their list included the following:

The team

- *Makes most of its daily decisions, such as assigning work, rotating jobs, scheduling vacations, etc.*
- *Performs the planning and scheduling of its work*
- *Handles routine administrative tasks formerly performed by supervisors*
- *Conducts its own quality audits*
- *Sets its own performance standards and measures its performance against them*
- *Develops goals aligned with the organization's goals*
- *Determines its own training needs*
- *Identifies improvements to its work processes*
- *Procures needed tools and materials*
- *Assumes responsibility for its work area layout and maintenance*
- *Conducts peer reviews in accordance with its own set of standards of performance*

The benefit of the list was that it gave a clear direction to new work teams that enabled them to map out a strategy for their development.

⊚ QUESTIONS TO CONSIDER

Boundaries and roles

Think about boundaries for a moment. In your work, do you clearly know the limits of what you can and cannot do? In what ways can boundaries actually give you more freedom? What boundaries could be clarified to make your work more focused and productive?

•

BOUNDARIES ENCOURAGE
CREATIVITY AND EXPLORATION

A research study we heard about demonstrates an interesting aspect of boundaries. A group of children was taken into an open field and told to play. The children huddled closely together, never venturing far from the group. The researchers then took them to a fenced-in area and the children used the entire space, exploring the far reaches of the playground.

If we use this example and relate it to organization behavior, we can find parallels. When people are unclear about boundaries, they tend to "huddle" in the safety of their known world or work space and its familiar structure and rules. However, if they are given boundaries that are clearly defined, the risk of venturing forth is less intimidating.

Perhaps the best example of this principle is demonstrated repeatedly by the work performed by problem-solving teams. When a problem exists in an organization, people will complain about it, believing they have little authority to affect it. When management authorizes a team to be formed to address the issue, the people assigned to the team are given well-defined boundaries, such as time, money, and resources, and they are expected and free to act within those boundaries.

★ **EXAMPLES**

Boundaries enable breakthroughs

One team from the agricultural equipment industry completely redesigned the company's core product, a tractor, in record time, having been allowed to bypass all the policies and administrative procedures that historically slowed the process.

•

Sales of the tractor had dropped significantly in recent years, but completely redesigning it under the company's normal process would have taken too long. So management selected a team of people from across the company and gave them the task of redesigning it in record time. To do this they were given the authority to bypass long-standing processes and procedures. The end result was a new tractor that was designed in about one-third of the normal time. But more importantly, it was a hit in the marketplace, adding much-needed revenue and profits to the bottom line.

Boundaries and growth

Another team at an electric utility company researched and solved a significant work-shift problem that had lowered productivity and annoyed workers and their families for years.

Frustrated by constant complaints about the nuclear power plant operators' shift schedule, the division vice president assembled a team of operators to work on it. To find the best solution, he gave the team a great amount of freedom to research the subject.

After six months of studying the problem, the team recommended a new schedule based on twelve-hour workdays. The vice president was happy with the recommendation; however, the team would need to convince the Nuclear Regulatory Commission, which was concerned about the long workdays and the possibility of workers sleeping on the job.

The operator team had researched its subject well, however, and was able to convince the commission that the new schedule would, in fact, improve the operators' energy, alertness, and attention to their task. The new shift schedule was approved. The commission was so impressed with the team's research and recommendations that it asked the team to make presentations to other electric utilities on what the operators had learned.

•

In both of these cases, breakthroughs were achieved because the boundaries (mainly policies and procedures) that had previously restricted creativity and action were removed and replaced by boundaries that allowed more freedom (clear goals and resources). People were allowed to behave and perform in ways that were forbidden under traditional policies but are encouraged in Next Level Teams.

The good news was that significant breakthroughs occurred, improving the organization in measurable ways. The bad news was—and remains—that constraints to creativity and innovation continue to exist. Administrative procedures and policies are so ingrained in our work systems that it takes a significant shift in our thinking to adjust, modify, or eliminate them. But when the shift is made, great results can be achieved.

Boundaries that restrict or hold back are like barbed wire. Boundaries that allow freedom are like rubber bands.

QUESTIONS TO CONSIDER

Boundaries and exploration

How do people in your organization react when asked to take on more responsibility, given the kinds of boundaries (policies and procedures) that exist today in your organization? How do you think people would respond if provided clear boundaries (goals and resources) within which to take responsible action to get desired results? Why would they react this way?

BOUNDARIES: A CAUTION

A primary purpose for moving to Next Level Teams is to create the freedom to act. So in this first step of the change process, boundaries should be defined that are not overly restrictive but at the same time not so wide as to inhibit people from taking action.

At the outset of the journey to the Next Level, it is better to err in the direction of more restrictive boundaries that create a small playing field for people. It is easier to widen a boundary and allow more freedom than to suddenly close it in because people have not been able to handle the scope of responsibility. It will also be difficult to identify all boundaries at the outset, so everyone should be very aware that the journey to Next Level Teams is, indeed, a journey. The process will need to be adapted as it evolves.

 EXAMPLES

Defining helpful boundaries

A case in point shows how an overly restrictive boundary inhibits progress. In a pharmaceutical manufacturing facility, a three-year-old self-directed work team had been making great strides in improving its work process. The team was flying along at a speed that outpaced the rest of the organization. When the team members needed to order a fabricated part for one of their new process improvements, they ran into a purchasing policy (constraint) that slowed them considerably. The cumbersome policy frustrated the team and was a source of considerable demotivation.

Boundaries that don't work

Another case illustrates the difficulty of drawing the boundaries too wide. At a television station, the president wanted to move quickly to a team environment. He immediately created teams and asked all teams to set goals for their work areas, which would be shared with him and others on the management team. After waiting two weeks for any team to come forward, he was disappointed to learn that no team had created any goals. When questionned, some people reported that they just did not know where to start— they felt overwhelmed with the broad definition of their task. Others reported being fearful of setting goals that were too ambitious since they knew that the management team had a history of punishing people who did not achieve their goals. Based on the history of management response and a lack of knowledge on how to proceed, the teams chose to do nothing.

*At an individual level, to be self-regulating is
to test and know our own boundaries—for example,
to establish where we give ourselves permission to act
and where we stop ourselves from acting.*

JILL JANOV

Turning restraints into guidelines

Think about what restrains your ability to be your best at work. What are some of the organization systems and procedures that tend to hold you back? How could these be changed without going too far too fast? What types of new boundaries could free you and help you to take focused action?

 EXAMPLES

Boundaries and the koi

A favorite fish collected by fish hobbyists is the Japanese carp, commonly known as the koi.

The fascinating thing about the koi is that if you keep it in a small fishbowl, it will grow to be only two or three inches long. But place the koi in a larger tank or small pond and it will reach six to ten inches.

If the koi is placed in a large pond, it may get as long as a foot and a half. However, when placed in a lake where it can really stretch out, it has the potential to reach a length up to three feet! The size of the fish is in direct relation to its environment.

This metaphor is appropriate for Next Level Teams because the "size" of people is also proportional to their environment. When you allow people to swim in a larger pond, so to speak, they grow in competence, character, and commitment.

Empowering people to swim in larger waters is the essence of a Next Level culture. Like the koi, people grow when the opportunity permits.

•

Remember, boundaries should tell people what they can do, not what they cannot do.

WILLIAM J. GRAHAM

FOUR

Act Like a Team to Promote Shared Involvement

At this point, it's time for your group to begin operating as a true team with a genuine sense of shared involvement.

The quality movement of the 1980s ushered in widespread use of employee involvement. People at all levels of organizations, especially those on the front lines, became involved in how to think about organization improvement. One of the primary methods for maximizing this involvement was the use of teams. It was shown repeatedly that collaboration in teams resulted in significant breakthroughs in problem solving and innovation, so teams were established as a means to achieving great results. Their use has continued to grow.

 EXAMPLES

The power of a team

In 1983, a management team of a large organization was struggling with a severe traffic problem on the road leading to the organization's location. The road crossed four miles of protected wetlands, so it could not be widened without significant environmental impact. Each morning the traffic leading to the site backed up the entire four-mile length of the road, adding an hour to commuting time. The resulting aggravation caused productivity to drop significantly.

Three years earlier, the management team had hired traffic consultants to solve the problem. Their work focused on a future widening of the road and looked promising, but their attempts to devise short-term solutions failed miserably.

As a last resort, management decided to assemble a team of people from the company to address short-term solutions. The ten-person team was composed of engineers, clerical personnel, line workers, and union representatives. This team met twice a week for a month, culminating in a series of recommendations that ultimately improved the traffic flow both into and out of the site.

The simplicity of the team's recommendations surprised management. For example, the team suggested that trucks be prohibited from making deliveries to the site between the hours of 6:00 a.m. and 9:00 a.m. Since many deliveries were made to the site at this time, this recommendation immediately removed some of the slowest, most cumbersome traffic clogging the road. Other recommendations also contributed to easing the problem. The result was almost instantaneous improvement in the traffic flow.

At the outset, the members of the management team had doubted that this new team could solve the problem. After all, experts had been studying it for three years. But in turning to their own people they found a solution. They tapped into the essence of true involvement and teamwork.

Given the freedom to brainstorm and experiment, people are endlessly innovative. And when people collaborate as a team, the innovative ideas multiply and yield powerful results.

•

The use of teams has grown in the workplace in direct proportion to the business needs of greater flexibility, rapid decision making, and faster innovation. Teams are part of a trend toward greater collaboration in the workplace. This trend is a response to the growing complexity and dynamism of work demands and has continued to yield positive results for more than two decades.

> *The best method of overcoming obstacles*
>
> *is the team method.*
>
> COLIN L. POWELL

 QUESTIONS TO CONSIDER

Successful teams

Think back to a team you were once a part of that you considered to be highly successful and highly rewarding. What were the characteristics of that team? What made it successful?

NEXT LEVEL TEAMS VERSUS WORK GROUPS

Unfortunately, few of us were taught to use team behaviors as a way to get things done when we were growing up. Both our schools and our workplaces have emphasized individual achievement, creating a system where few people appreciate the need for collaboration and real teamwork.

The traditional work structure operates through central decision making, with information and work direction cascading down through the various management levels. In this kind of system, work groups carry out the decisions and direction provided by managers, and they seldom exercise discretionary thinking.

In the new system of work, Next Level Teams carry out tasks similar to work groups but exercise greater discretionary authority when making decisions about how the team operates and how the work is performed. These teams become partners with management in creating highly effective work processes that achieve great results.

It may seem like a play on words, but there are fundamental differences between a work group and a Next Level Team. Let us explore these differences a little further.

The Work Group

The work group was designed to accomplish work through a supervisor. Each person in the group is assigned a task by the supervisor and is responsible for the successful completion of that task.

In a work group system, the center of activity is the supervisor. The supervisor sets goals, plans the work, controls the workflow, determines staffing, evaluates group and individual performance, makes decisions for the group, resolves conflicts, and conducts meetings. In the extreme, workers do only what they are told to do by the supervisor, thus limiting utilization of the workers' knowledge, experience, and motivation. Results that follow also tend to be limited.

Employee Involvement and the Desire for Greater Efficiency

During the quality movement of the 1980s, managers found that involving frontline employees in problem solving generated a broader spectrum of solutions. An increased need for innovation demanded that more brainpower be focused on the problems of the organization. Group problem solving grew in response to this need.

As the work group's problem-solving skills were used more broadly, it became apparent that frontline employees were capable of greater authority and responsibility. Work groups were evolving into self-regulated units, assuming more control of their daily work and more responsibility for outcomes. When teams were fully self-directing, they planned and scheduled their own work, made assignments within the team, initiated improvements to their work processes, set goals and objectives, performed quality checks, made staffing decisions, set work standards, evaluated team member performance, and more.

To succeed, the people in this new type of work group had to rely more on each other's skills and abilities, communicate more openly, and develop a greater sense of interdependence. When organizations began reducing levels of management in the 1990s to create greater efficiency, make better use of technology, and respond to global challenges, an even greater need for highly effective teams developed.

The Next Level Team

In today's fast-paced and extremely complex global business environment, the work team needs to evolve again to become a highly effective Next Level Team. The need today is to establish a true partnership between the team and the organization, built around extensive information sharing and wide boundaries of authority that allow more freedom for teams to take action. In a Next Level Team, members take ownership of the responsibility for continually developing themselves and improving their work processes. Team members understand that the organization succeeds or fails depending on how effectively they and their leadership perform the work. Next Level Teams operate as integral parts of the organization, making full use of the knowledge, experience, and motivation of team members to impact team and organizational results in powerful and effective ways.

STARTING A NEXT LEVEL TEAM HAS ITS CHALLENGES

New teams—and even mature teams at times—tend to struggle as they grow. Issues related to how the work is performed and how team members relate to each other come quickly to the forefront.

A *Business Week* magazine article discussed steps that were being taken by the Los Angeles Unified School District to overhaul its teaching process and introduce team concepts. In this article, a comment was made that gives us a clue as to why we struggle with teamwork.

The district's assistant superintendent stated, "In the business world, sharing responsibility for a project is called teamwork. In classrooms, the way we teach today, it's called cheating."[1]

Most people in the workplace were reared in a school system that rewarded individual accomplishment. When they entered the workplace, the resulting learned behaviors were reinforced by a similar system of individual rewards, such as promotions, merit raises, and forced rankings. Little emphasis was placed on collaboration and teamwork.

This system led to behaviors that focused on the self and one's personal accomplishments. When team concepts were introduced into the organizational fabric, different behaviors and skills were required. Such a change brings with it difficulty and discomfort.

Imagine a singer who has sung solo his entire career being asked to participate in a quartet. The singer must now learn new techniques, harmonize with the others, respect their needs, and communicate extensively. A different set of skills is needed that may initially generate feelings of inadequacy, insecurity, and, sometimes, incompetence. The accompanying discomfort is real.

In cooperative situations, others are depending on

you to succeed. In competitive situations,

others hope to see you fail.

CHARLES DYGERT

MAKING EFFECTIVE USE OF OUR DIFFERENCES

The strength of any team is in the diverse talents, skills, values, and personalities of its members. Yet the same qualities that create its strengths also fuel its problems.

For instance, the personality traits that allow one person to initiate breakthrough ideas and another person to turn those ideas into practical realities (both important traits for the team) are often the same traits that cause much disagreement and conflict between those same people. The detailed, practical person may frequently be angered by the idea person's flights of fancy. And the idea person may feel stymied by the practical person's need for detail and analysis.

•

Since we were not reared with an understanding of collaboration, our emotions will usually hinder us from seeing the benefits of our differences, and this can be a significant and ongoing source of problems for the team.

◎ **QUESTIONS TO CONSIDER**

Team challenges

In your experiences with teams, what challenges have held them back from being their best? What are the challenges today that hold back your work team from becoming a Next Level Team? Are you making effective use of the differences of team members?

> *The quickest way to kindle a fire is to*
> *rub two opposing opinions together.*

UNKNOWN

TEAM BASICS: THE FOUR QUESTIONS A NEXT LEVEL TEAM MUST ANSWER

Research on teams for almost one hundred years has shown that there are four primary elements of highly successful teams. To develop your Next Level Team properly and keep it on track, you need to ask and answer four questions:

1. Do we have a common purpose or mission?
2. Do we have agreed-upon operating processes?
3. Do we have shared operating principles?
4. Do we understand and appreciate our different roles?

Let's look at these in a little more detail.

Team Mission

Most teams that fail do so because team members lack clarity and alignment about their mission. The mission is what the team does, its purpose for existing. New teams or teams in trouble should clearly define what they do to each member's satisfaction. The more clearly this mission is defined, the more able team members will be to take the appropriate actions to accomplish it.

It is generally accepted that the reason NASA was so effective in building a world-class space agency during the 1960s is because the mission was crystal clear to every one of the thousands of people involved. The mission, as articulated by President Kennedy, was "to put a man on the moon by the end of the decade."

Operating Processes

An operating process gives a team structure as to how it will operate while completing its task or tasks. It tells the team how decisions will be made as they relate to important issues. In actuality, the team may have multiple operating processes to accomplish various tasks. To be effective, a team must have clear and agreed-upon operating processes. Examples of team operating processes include

- The steps involved in manufacturing a product
- The steps involved in handling a customer complaint
- The process for resolving a conflict among team members
- The process for scheduling vacations

Operating Principles

Operating principles determine how team members will work together, particularly how they will treat each other. Teams frequently struggle with the "people" aspects of running a team because members lack a common view of how they want to work together. Operating principles are guidelines that help team members put into action the values they share in terms of how they work together. For example, a code of conduct of one team read as follows:

- Team members will treat each other with dignity and respect at all times.

- Team members will share equal responsibility for the outcome of team accomplishments.

- Team members will respect others by being on time for meetings, avoiding demeaning language, and acknowledging the diversity of opinions.

- Team members will have fun as much as possible.

Team Member Roles

Team members have both *formal* and *informal* roles to play on a team. The formal roles are usually defined by work responsibilities, such as electrician, plumber, apprentice, clerk, accountant, scheduler, coordinator, team leader, and so forth. The informal roles are defined by the natural skills and talents each team member brings to the team process. For example, some team members have a natural ability in mediating conflicts. Some are good meeting managers. Some have good detail skills, while others are better at generating ideas. Some members have a natural energizing quality that brings life to the team, while others are more steady and practical, bringing the needed glue that holds the team together technically and administratively.

These abilities should be discussed to identify people's natural talents and how they might best be used. The team should also attempt to identify missing skills and their implications.

 QUESTIONS TO CONSIDER

Team basics

Think about the team basics above as they apply to your team. Does your team apply all four of these basics? Frequently teams struggle because one or more of these elements is missing from the team's functioning. What about your team as it is today?

TEAMWORK: A REQUIRED BUSINESS SKILL

The ability to operate successfully in a team environment is rapidly moving to the forefront of required business skills. The use of teams in the workplace has grown and continues to grow, not because of some human relations initiative, but because of the realities of succeeding in an increasingly competitive and complex business environment.

People working together in task forces, problem-solving teams, product development teams, and committees bring a collective wisdom that significantly multiplies the ability to innovate. Add to this the commitment that develops as a result of a sense of shared involvement and you can begin to understand the enormous potential of collaboration and teamwork.

•

Teamwork is the ability to work together toward a common vision. The ability to direct individual accomplishment toward organizational objectives. It is the fuel that allows common people to attain uncommon results.

UNKNOWN

Accelerate
the Change

FIVE

Share More Information to Enhance Trust

You have now completed step 1 in becoming a Next Level Team. You have begun to use information to build responsibility, clarify boundaries to create focused action, and act like a team to promote shared involvement.

In any process of change, frustration is inevitable. It is at this point that people sometimes feel like giving up on the change. Yet we have learned that it is at this very point that the energy of frustration can be refocused and used to accelerate the change to Next Level Teams.

FRUSTRATION IS TYPICAL, BUT IT IS A POWERFUL SOURCE OF ENERGY

We often hear people express frustration at how long change takes. Once a commitment is made to move forward with creating a Next Level Team, everyone wants to get there fast. We want to accelerate the change and get to the goal.

The problem is that changing from the traditional view of the manager as decision maker and team members as doers to collaborative Next Level Teams means using different skills.

•

Along the way you are also learning a new way to view responsibility, decision making and teamwork. Feelings of frustration and discouragement are typical during such a significant change process. The excitement people feel as they begin to learn Next Level skills is almost always replaced with questions: How long will this take? Can we really do this? Will these changes actually work? This is the time to explore ways to use the energy of frustration to accelerate the transition to Next Level Teams.

 EXAMPLES

Dealing with frustration

One of our consulting experiences brought this point home very clearly. After we had been working with a company for about six months, we saw many signs of discouragement from both leaders and team members. People were heard to say, "This teamwork stuff will never work. Our leaders don't really want us to take action on our own."

At the same time, leaders were heard to say, "When will our people begin to take action? They know we want them to be empowered. What is the holdup?" It was clear that the change to teams was in trouble; it was quickly becoming just another "flavor of the month" management effort.

Our next step was to explain that such frustration and discouragement were not uncommon—in fact, they were to be expected in a change effort. Any time you are learning new skills, you will experience some discouragement. We also explained how people in other companies had experienced exactly the same problems. We also told them that people do get through this tough stage of change.

The response was surprising. Leaders and team members began to talk openly about their frustration and discouragement. They *listened to each other and began to talk about how they could deal with their problems. Some said, "If those other companies could handle these problems, so can we. In fact, we can do it even better than they did." What resulted was a renewed energy for change and an acceleration of the process.*

FIVE REASONS FOR FRUSTRATION

When incorporating Next Level Team concepts, frustrations may surface for a number of predictable reasons:

1. *Initial expectations are not in line with reality.* Almost everyone, from senior management to team members, tends to underestimate what is involved in making the change to Next Level Teams.

2. *People are concerned that the process will fail.* Some people harbor a concern that the entire process is doomed to failure from the outset. The first sign of any problems confirms this belief, leading to disillusionment about whether change is possible in their company.

3. *Guidance and understanding are inadequate.* Team members wonder if they will ever be freed to use their talents and judgment, while leaders wonder if the team members will ever take responsibility for results.

4. *People fear personal failure.* Both team members and leaders fear that they will appear incompetent in a changed culture. These fears will usually remain unspoken, but tend to manifest themselves in inaction and indecision.

5. *Training for dealing with team development issues is lacking.* Without proper preparation, most teams will be unprepared for the normal stages of team development, which always include some bumps along the way.

•

These typical but unexpected problems can result in disruption and disillusionment about the whole team idea.

Frustrations you may feel

Change brings with it inherent discomfort and challenges. You may be feeling some of these frustrations as your team moves to the Next Level. Use the list of five reasons for frustration above to stimulate your thinking. What is causing you to doubt the move to Next Level Teams? What frustrations are you feeling now?

FOCUS ON THE BENEFITS FOR TEAM MEMBERS

During difficult periods in the change process, it helps team members to focus on the benefits they will gain from working in a Next Level Team. All too often organizations and team leaders focus too much on the ways in which the organization will benefit, as though that is what matters most to the team members. Of course, the reality is that team members want to know how they will benefit personally. Many benefits will result from sharing increasing amounts of information; team members feeling frustration need to be reminded of these benefits.

For example, team members with more information benefit by having more control over their work. In addition, gaining access to more information tells team members that they are valued members of the organization. Having more information also helps team members feel a sense of pride and ownership unlike anything they have experienced in a traditional work group setting.

•

Team leaders also benefit from greater information sharing. Leaders benefit by having team members who share responsibility for achieving results and goals. They also benefit by having the opportunity to focus their energies on higher value-added work. These significant benefits will ultimately lead to greater team performance and job satisfaction.

Sharing information and listening to the benefits that will ultimately accrue refocuses people on the positive outcomes of becoming a Next Level Team. In turn, this information sharing enhances the trust that is needed to move forward.

⊚ **QUESTIONS TO CONSIDER**

Benefits you already see

As you think about the movement of your team to the Next Level, what benefits can you already see happening (at least a little)? What benefits seem to be happening that are good for you, your team, your team leader, and the organization?

SHARING MORE SENSITIVE INFORMATION

With the benefits of change to Next Level Teams in focus, the frustration people may be feeling can be redirected as a force for change. By sharing more sensitive information about the organization, leaders can build trust and responsibility. For example, leaders can show they trust the team by sharing information about critical issues facing the organization, including information about loss of revenue, quality issues, or complaints from customers.

Providing information to team members about these kinds of problems tells them they are trusted colleagues. Indeed, they are seen as part of the solution rather than part of the problem.

•

Sharing all the facts is a powerful way to improve understanding and create feelings of trust, which are then substituted for feelings of frustration with the change.

Leaders should also share information about mistakes that have been made, taking care not to place blame. This will make team members feel a greater desire to contribute ideas and take on responsibility. When people are given more responsibility, it is natural for the fear of failure to increase because mistakes are more likely. In a Next Level Team, everyone needs to feel it is safe to make mistakes and to learn from them. People naturally have a desire to try out new ideas that can improve team performance, but leaders must be willing to reward risk taking rather than punishing mistakes that occur as a result of trying new ideas.

 EXAMPLES

Turning mistakes into opportunities

One company went so far as to place bells in each office. When a mistake was made, someone would ring a bell to announce the mistake and simultaneously to mark the search for learning from the mistake.

What the leaders tried to do was to create an atmosphere where mistakes were celebrated because they meant people were taking the risks of responsibility and innovation and because the people were providing opportunities for learning.

What they found was that people did make more mistakes than in the past, but they also generated more innovative ideas, which resulted in improved performance of the work units. Mistakes became effective means for learning how to improve team performance.

SOLICITING INFORMATION FROM TEAM MEMBERS

When we begin to change to a culture that shares and uses information more effectively and respects the learning that comes from mistakes, team members also become aware of information they can share. Team leaders can tap into this information as a source of both ideas and energy by encouraging open dialogue about important issues. Of course, this openness means that everyone (leaders included) must be ready to face issues head-on. This is a time to foster real candor, rather than trying to decide what people should and should not hear. In such an environment, leaders may occasionally find themselves on the "hot seat" as difficult questions are raised by team members and need to be addressed by the leader. But this also provides the opportunity to make huge advances in building trust and responsibility.

 EXAMPLES

Listening to team feedback

One of the most interesting meetings we ever observed was where a leadership team in a computer company sat in front of a group of team members responding to their questions about the business. These team members were well informed about business results, and they wanted to know why the plant's performance results were declining.

They asked some very pointed questions about resources, strategic decisions, and cost containment decisions that management had made. It was clear that they felt these decisions had not been well thought through.

The most amazing aspect, though, was the response of the leaders to these "attacks." They all remained very calm and responded to the team members' concerns, even acknowledging that some of the decisions had not been the best.

They invited the employees to offer suggestions and to work with them to develop better ways to combat the competitive pressures from the marketplace. What followed, long after the meeting, was an energy that helped the company deal effectively with many of its problems in a manner that involved employees and managers working together as team members.

 QUESTIONS TO CONSIDER

Accelerating change with more information sharing

More and more sharing of information helps build greater trust, especially if more sensitive information is shared. Two-way communication helps people feel more valued and critical to team and organization success. What kinds of additional information could help your team be more productive? How could your team make good use of mistakes to learn how to improve results? What information could your team begin sharing with the team leader that would be helpful?

USING MEASUREMENTS AS INFORMATION TO ACCELERATE CHANGE

Any time we do something, there is a result. If we swing a bat at a ball, we can see the result immediately—a hit or a miss. We also see the effectiveness of the hit—the ball may go far or not. This immediate feedback gives us the ability to make adjustments quickly and become proficient at the task.

But what if we could not see the results of our effort? What if we were blindfolded and simply told when to swing? And

•

when we missed the ball, the coach yelled at us to try harder? Eventually, frustration, disillusionment, and anger would set in from the lack of progress.

The same thing occurs when people perform tasks at work but are unable to see the results of their work. This is especially critical during times of change. When your team is acquiring new roles, skills, and knowledge, it is important for the team to see its results quickly. Information that relates to measures of performance can be really effective at this point in the change process. Let's look at two examples.

Sharing increasing amounts of information is important during times of frustration. It gives people a sense of the progress they are making and enhances a sense of trust.

 EXAMPLES

The administrative team and the new copier

An administrative team at a New Jersey utility had analyzed one of its work processes and found real inefficiencies. Simply put, the team determined that the lack of copying machines in the office was causing significant delay time for each team member and others who used the existing machine. The one machine on the floor was far from their location and the waiting time at the machine was excessive.

The team prepared a presentation to request that a new copying machine be purchased and located nearer to them. Some of the team members, however, anguished over the recommendation because the new machine would cost the company $25,000 and might appear to management as though they were just complaining without real cause.

One of the members suggested measuring the total effect of the current situation by analyzing the walk time to the old machine and the delay time in waiting to use it. Previously, the team members had never done such an analysis, so attaching costs to their actions was new territory for them.

Their analysis showed that the yearly loss in productivity of team members was three times the cost of the new machine, or a return on investment of three to one. This immediately excited the team members as they were able to make a change that improved their work lives and performance and also made a cost-effective decision for the company. Their presentation was so well prepared that management immediately approved the purchase of the new machine.

Effective performance appraisals

A utility company in Florida realized the need to change its performance appraisal process to be more consistent with a culture of partnership between leaders and team members. During initial training about the new process, data was collected that measured perceptions of the effectiveness of setting goals, coaching employees, and evaluating performance.

After about a year, when people felt some discouragement that the changes were not that significant, data was collected again on the same three measurements. The results showed significant improvement in setting goals and evaluating performance. The data also identified the need for more focus on the coaching step in the process.

The leadership of the company took the time to celebrate the progress that had been made in a meaningful display of public praise and recognition. Everyone felt good to know that progress was being made, and all were energized to continue working to-

•

gether to improve the coaching partnership. In subsequent sessions, team members and their leaders alike brought up ideas for improving and solidifying a more effective performance management system.

These two stories illustrate the power of using measurements to accelerate change. The first story demonstrates the power of people having facts about problems. Armed with valid information, the team was motivated to study and prepare a proposal that dealt with the problem in a responsible fashion. A critical problem was solved, and the team members felt great about their contribution. The second story demonstrates how measurements can be used to help everyone mark progress toward a goal. This story also illustrates how praise for progress can be linked to measurements and can keep people energized for change. In short, measurements help people use their abilities to impact results and see the ongoing benefits of their efforts. Measurements also provide opportunities for praising progress. And the result is accelerated change through reduced frustration.

 QUESTIONS TO CONSIDER

Making better use of measurements

Think about how measurements could help tap into your team's ideas and motivation. How could measurements be better used to assess progress toward goals? How could measurements provide more opportunities to praise the progress of the team and its members? What measurements could be used more effectively with your team? Could new measurements of performance motivate your team?

•

INFORMATION SHARING MOVES THE TEAM
FROM FRUSTRATION TO CHANGE

As they move into step 2 of the change to Next Level Teams, leaders need to share not only more information but also more sensitive information. Why? Because this sharing of information helps reduce the frustration that comes with change by demonstrating a high level of trust between management and the workforce. It sends a powerful message that everyone is working together toward the same end.

As we have noted, information sharing is not simply a "top down" process. Frontline team members need to understand that the information they possess about the workings of the business is critical for managers to aid them in making good decisions about work processes and even the future of the organization. Therefore, open sharing of information from the bottom up is critical, too. Even bad news is good when shared because it opens up a dialogue that can lead to problem solving and enhanced trust between leaders and team members.

·

Some day, on the corporate balance sheet, there will be

an entry which reads, "Information"; for in most cases,

the information is more valuable than the

hardware which processes it.

GRACE MURRAY HOPPER

SIX

Widen the Boundaries to Promote Greater Freedom for Action

As the team moves forward and encounters frustration, it is easy for team members and leaders to lose sight of the vision of a Next Level Team and how it contributes to getting great results. They tend to see only the problems of taking on more responsibility and forget about the rewards of involvement and ownership. At this point, teams need to be reminded what Next Level Teams do and to be inspired by their benefits. This is the time to review the team's goals. Organizational goals—even department goals—can be too broad for practical use by most teams and their members. Such broad goals must be converted into images more directly related to the team's work.

Well-defined team goals help define boundaries and reenergize the team, especially if the goals are developed in a collaborative manner. With more information, team members can see the need for goals that yield important results, fix problems, create innovations, or move projects along. By being involved in a collaborative process of setting clear team goals, people begin to feel a real sense of freedom and responsibility that translates into a feeling of ownership for accomplishing tasks in an efficient manner.

EXAMPLES

Setting team goals

An information services company took a rather bold step at this stage of the process. Senior leadership took the position that employees with increased information at their disposal could now identify and define some of their own goals in collaboration with their leaders. Of the five to eight performance goals that were typical for teams, the leaders instructed members to try to develop three to four of those goals themselves.

At first, team members were confused, but they quickly came to like the idea, since it used their input and gave them a sense of ownership and power to affect results. The team leaders liked it as well, because it helped team members share the responsibility of identifying and defining the goals that were critical to the performance of the business unit. What followed was a collaborative discussion among team members during which team goals were refined to be what they called "POWER goals," that is, goals that are Pinpointed, Owned, Well-defined, Energizing, and Resourced.

THE IMPORTANCE OF TEAM GOALS

As this example suggests, team goals are important because they engage team members and team leaders in a dialogue that

All good performance starts with clear goals.

not only establishes the goals but also helps build the team as a unit. Most people have had far more experience with individual goals than with team goals as work has tended to be built around individual responsibility. By asking team members to focus on their team's performance and determine where performance improvement goals should be set, team leaders gain valuable insight from many sets of eyes, rather than just their own. At this stage of the change process, it is appropriate to ask teams to think of ways they can better contribute to working more efficiently and effectively. Now that the teams have access to critical organizational information, clearer goals can be set.

As a team sets goals, it is critical to create goals that are truly useful, meaningful, and motivating. To work well for a team, the goals need to be **POWER** goals—that is, goals that provide answers to five key questions:

Pinpointed: "What exactly are we trying to
              accomplish?"

Owned: "What's in it for us, and can we buy into
              this responsibility?"

Well-defined: "How can we assess and measure our
              progress?"

Energizing: "Is this goal realistic yet challenging?"

Resourced: "Are we clear on the resources available to
              us for this task?"[2]

QUESTIONS TO CONSIDER

Setting team goals

Think about your team and the kinds of tasks for which you are responsible. Now think about the information your team has at hand that could help you focus on some challenges and opportunities for the team. What are some new areas of focus for which your team could begin to set POWER goals and take responsibility for achieving them?

WIDENING BOUNDARIES BY
SETTING PERSONAL DEVELOPMENT GOALS

In addition to setting performance goals, teams can also focus on skill development and career enhancement goals. Next Level Teams nurture the development of new skills and abilities so that the team can tackle critical goals and make team decisions that generate great results. At the same time, Next Level Teams offer people exciting opportunities for personal growth and development that can positively impact their careers.

For example, people who aspire to positions of greater responsibility may need to develop leadership skills, presentation skills, conflict management skills, or decision-making skills. In Next Level Teams, people can find opportunities to use and master these kinds of skills. In a Next Level Team, it is important to determine what skills you need to develop, not only to help the team perform, but also to help you succeed in your career.

 EXAMPLES

Values as goals

One interesting case in point on goal setting comes from a company whose leaders wanted people to focus attention not only on performance goals but also on goals related to values. Realizing that goals are set but values are lived, the leaders wanted to ensure that people kept values in mind as they worked together on meaningful goals. For example, if one value is "better relationships between departments," people might set a goal around the question, "What am I going to do this year to improve the rela-

tionships between my department and others?" Or if a value is for people to "grow in skills and abilities," a goal might be, "What new skill am I going to learn this year, and how will I demonstrate the new skill?"

The leaders found that focusing on such goals gave people real clarity and accountability about what to accomplish (performance goals) and how to work together (values goals). When coupled with an expectation that leaders would coach and help people achieve their goals, these teams were able to work together in new ways that made better use of their talents, energy, and motivation.

 QUESTIONS TO CONSIDER

Personal development goals

Think for a moment about your own personal development and your career aspirations. What are some areas of your work where you would like to learn new skills? Are there some goals that would be valuable to your team that also relate to how you work together?

WIDENING THE BOUNDARIES TO INCLUDE ORGANIZATIONAL ISSUES

Another way to turn a team's frustration into action during step 2 of the change process is to expand the range of decisions the team can make to include organizational issues. This expansion of opportunity sends a clear signal of support and encouragement for the team to continue moving toward the Next Level. When people feel their ideas count and they have responsibility for significant decisions, they feel valued, which turns discouragement into development.

During step 1, the purpose of boundaries was to create a focus for the action of team members. The goal was to start teams making decisions that were not too complex but that could be used to help team members and leaders understand the power of focusing action through boundaries. Now it is time for the team to begin making decisions that can have a greater impact on organizational results. Examples of such critical decisions are

- Determining training needs
- Scheduling and controlling production
- Managing suppliers

During this process, teams may find that some organizational systems operate more like barbed wire—holding people in—rather than expanding like rubber bands as people grow in Next Level Team skills.

Let's be bold and consider one of the most critical organizational decision issues that often derails Next Level Teams. Performance appraisals and the way they are managed clearly affect the way people behave in an organization. It is not unusual to find inconsistencies between the existing appraisal procedures and the kind of performance appraisal process that would support Next Level Teams. When team members have more access to information, they will no doubt recognize the inconsistencies.

Some important questions can be asked about the performance appraisal system to stimulate thinking about needed changes:

- How do people—both leaders and team members— like the existing process?

•

- How many people dread the time when appraisals take place?
- Does the process punish or develop people?
- Is the appraisal a partnership between leaders and team members?
- Does the process support a focus on team goals and team performance?

In most organizations, we have found that people answer these questions negatively. The performance appraisal form used in most organizations is disliked and seen as punitive. People dread performance evaluation time since it is full of unpleasant surprises. The process focuses on evaluating individuals for pay decisions and does not focus on team performance. While such a system may have worked in an organization run like a management hierarchy, it will not work with Next Level Teams. Something has got to change.

EXAMPLES

The utility company and team appraisals

In one southeastern utility company that wanted to implement reliance on self-directed teams, training was begun to help everyone understand the new direction. The management team provided strong support for giving the teams more information and the authority to make critical business decisions. Everything appeared to be moving ahead quite well until it came time for annual performance appraisals.

One day during a training session, one of the workers said to the instructor, "Have you ever seen our performance appraisal forms?" A bit surprised, the instructor responded that he had not.

The team member said, "Well, it contradicts everything you are teaching us and what we are trying to do!"

The ensuing discussion revealed that the performance appraisal form was a list of items about each person that the supervisor was to check off using a five-point scale. The items included (1) Has a positive work attitude, (2) Completes work in a timely fashion, (3) Responds well to requests from supervisors, and (4) Is cooperative with others. But the real kicker was that after rating each person in a work group, the supervisor had to rank the people from best to worst in the group—so much for teamwork. This appraisal format had been used for a number of years. At worst, it created unnecessary competition among team members if the supervisor took it seriously. At best, the supervisor ignored the ranking and everyone viewed the process as a joke. It did nothing to support teams that made decisions and took responsibility for accomplishing goals.

Fortunately, when the senior vice president of the division was presented with this information, he made sure the process was altered to exclude the ranking and to include both team and individual assessments.

"BUT OUR TEAM CAN'T AFFECT ORGANIZATIONAL POLICY!"

At this point, you might be thinking that your team has no ability to affect the organization's policies. Management must set policies and procedures. Let's return to the central theme of the previous chapter—information sharing, including information sharing from employees to management. Frequently, managers in an organization are unaware that policies are inconsistent with an effort to change the organization. In the case above, the leaders were oblivious to the fact that the performance appraisal process promoted competition among team members rather than focusing on teamwork. Only when people on the teams brought it to management's attention was the process changed.

Moving to Next Level Teams means that everyone is responsible for outcomes. Team members need to recognize and expose processes and policies that get in the way of progress. When an organization is truly moving toward Next Level Teams, open dialogue and questioning of procedures and processes are welcome and invited. Teams have more power than they realize. Many times we have seen teams affect policies and processes, usually when they provide a solid analysis and effective presentation of the problem. The message to team members at this point in the change process is to always be vigilant for things that are blocking progress.

⊚ **QUESTIONS TO CONSIDER**

Problems with organizational systems

Think about your organization's policies and procedures, especially those that relate to team performance. Which policies and procedures do you feel need to be changed to better support the principles of Next Level Teams—involvement, empowerment, collaboration, and team responsibility?

WIDER BOUNDARIES TURN DISCOURAGEMENT INTO DEVELOPMENT

The valley of discouragement through which all teams must pass on the journey to the Next Level can be a difficult stage. It is somewhat paradoxical that by giving people more responsibility—by widening and deepening the boundaries—

•

this discouragement can be converted into the development of the team. Giving responsibility works because it addresses the underlying key concern of both managers and team members.

Boundaries create freedom—they keep you in bounds. Without them you could end up running in the grand-stands rather than on the playing field.

Deep down, managers fear that teams will not be able to reach the Next Level, where they can really impact results. And team members fear either that they will not be successful as Next Level Teams or that management will stop this change before positive results are achieved.

By expanding the boundaries just a little—and then some more—during this second step of change, leaders as well as team members are given the chance to see positive results without stretching either party beyond what they can yet handle.

•

Of course we all have our limits, but how can you possibly find your boundaries unless you explore as far and as wide as you possibly can? I would rather fail in an attempt at something new and uncharted than safely succeed in a repeat of something I have done.

A. E. HOTCHNER

SEVEN

Make Team Decisions to Create a Sense of Power

At this point your team is probably beginning to feel a sense of power that may be new for most team members. You have information that has never before been in your hands, and you have begun to work with clearly defined team goals. With these two skills developing, the change to a Next Level Team is ready for real acceleration. What is needed to make that happen is for your team to begin making *team decisions*. That means actually making decisions together, not just recommending and then having the team leader make the decision. Let us consider the elements and power of team decision making.

MORE DECISION-MAKING AUTHORITY FOR THE TEAM

As we have noted in the two previous chapters connected to step 2 of the change process, moving to Next Level Teams is often beset with feelings of discouragement. These feelings of discouragement tend to arise from the fact that people can feel alone with their self-doubts, even though others on the team have the same feelings. Even with more information and wider boundaries, some of the concerns that may still be going through people's minds are

- I wonder if others feel as awkward and strange about these changes as I do.
- I used to know what was happening and how to do my job. But now I sometimes feel lost and unsure about how to do my work in a team.
- I'm not sure I have the skills that are going to be needed in a Next Level Team.
- Some people on our team seem so ready to change, but I'm not ready yet. Or I'm ready to change but everybody else seems to be dragging their feet.

To combat these lingering feelings, it is time to actually expand the team members' decision-making authority to build confidence in their abilities. The team members need to learn how to use the information they now receive and the boundaries that are defined to guide them in making team decisions.

Habit is habit, and not to be flung out of the window,

but coaxed downstairs a step at a time.

MARK TWAIN

ENLISTING NATURAL TALENTS
OF TEAM MEMBERS

A good starting point for learning to make team decisions is to consider the roles that team members can play at this stage of the change. Your team is not yet fully developed. It is not yet functioning at the full capacity of a Next Level Team. Indeed, your team is not yet ready to make the more complex decisions that will come a little later.

One key characteristic of a Next Level Team is a feeling of ownership and pride in making important decisions. But team members also feel the pressures that traditionally were felt by their leader. With your team still developing its skills and feeling the early pressures of ownership, discouragement and concern about failure are inevitable. The team continues to need guidance and direction from the team leader about what to do and how to do it. Yet the team needs to begin making its own decisions to accelerate the change.

Team members help each other move through this stage by encouraging each person's natural abilities. The diversity of team members ensures that a broad range of talents, skills, and competencies are represented on the team. When an issue arises, one or more team members can usually step forward with the skills to handle it, though they will likely need encouragement to do so.

Skills such as facilitating team meetings, making joint decisions, resolving conflicts, listening effectively, encouraging others, being sure everyone is heard, and keeping team discussions focused on the issue at hand are all important for effective team functioning. Usually, some team members will have abilities in one or more of these areas. They can lead and teach others these skills so that gradually everyone can acquire new and important team functioning abilities.

The team assets inventory

In one company in the information services industry, the teams made a conscious effort to identify the talents of each team member. They called it a "team assets inventory," and the result was made public to all team members. When issues arose that related to a particular expertise, the appropriate person was encouraged by the team leader to take a leadership role in working on that issue.

Still, the team members were reluctant to use their talents until others on the team began to add their words of encouragement. With the stage set for sharing leadership, more and more team members began to recognize when they could make a contribution. They began to step forward, sometimes with ideas or suggestions and at other times simply with words of encouragement and praise for others. As a result, the teams began to function at a much higher level.

QUESTIONS TO CONSIDER

Taking an inventory of team talents

Think about the talents, skills, and abilities you possess that can be of value to your team at this stage of development. Be sure to include abilities such as mediating conflicts, building relationships, solving problems, running meetings, keeping logs, taking notes, using math or science skills, writing, summarizing discussions, and introducing new ideas. What skills and talents do others on your team have that could help your team function well?

EXPANDING THE RANGE OF TEAM MEMBERS' ROLES THROUGH TRAINING

You and other team members will possess many skills and abilities that can help the team function well, and you are now aware of what some of those skills are. It may also be apparent that team members need to acquire some skills for better team functioning.

Perhaps your team is struggling with frequent arguments, an inability to reach agreements, poor meeting management, lack of technical skills, quality control, listening, praising, and so on. If so, your team should look for help or training to acquire or enhance the needed skills.

 EXAMPLES

Developing team skills

A financial services group engaged us in a year-long effort to train their teams in a just-in-time manner. They constantly addressed team skill needs and designed training to teach those skills. The teams used these new skills and let us know where they were having problems. By the end of the year, the teams had become quite good at team communications, consensus decision making, conflict resolution, support of each other, and sharing of leadership. Their results reflected the application of these skills through demonstrated performance improvements using a variety of measurements.

•

REMOVING OBSTACLES THROUGH
EFFECTIVE TEAM PROCESSES

At this stage it is helpful to look at how your team handles internal issues. If your team is struggling with any aspect of its functioning, such as conflict resolution, consensus reaching, meeting management, or problem solving, it is useful to determine if a specific process might alleviate the problem.

For example, when working more independently than in the past and because change in itself is usually uncomfortable, some teams struggle with how to handle conflict. If this is an issue, team members should set aside time to develop a process for handling conflict. Everyone needs to recognize that conflict in team decision making is actually a good thing—it brings out different ideas, opinions, and perspectives. And it is a source of energy—people do not have conflict over matters that they don't care about. The challenge is not to eliminate conflict; the challenge is to channel that energy into better decisions.

 EXAMPLES

The conflict resolution process

In an organization in the retail food industry, teams agreed on a specific course of action to follow when conflict arose. First, they would discuss how each member of the team felt about the issue and why. Second, they would discuss what would have to change for each team member to feel comfortable. Third, they would focus on what they were willing to do as individuals to reach a comfort zone. And finally, they would move to a resolution of the conflict that came as close as possible to a win-win situation for all parties involved.

•

This conflict resolution process gave them a framework for dealing with conflict in a constructive, less emotional manner. It allowed them to use the conflict to explore alternatives and to focus the energy on a solution that worked well for everyone.

WHAT MAKES TEAMS SUCCEED OR FAIL?

Below is a list that compares characteristics that make teams and their environments either stagnate or thrive. This list is based on our years of observing and working with teams. If your team can be described by the words in the "Stagnate" column, it is not moving toward the Next Level. Only by operating in line with the words in the "Thrive" column can a team move to Next Level status.

Stagnate	Thrive
Unclear purpose	Stated, clear-cut mission
Dysfunctional behavior	Shared operating principles
Personality clashes	Valuing of differences
Emotional conflict	Healthy disagreement
Restricted authority	Empowerment to take action
Management indifference	Management enthusiasm
Verbal support	Visible support
Fear of failure	Confidence, risktaking
Hidden information	Open communication
Fear of self-analysis	Continual evaluation
Untrained members	Trained members
Selfish attitudes	Liberal praise
"Work is a chore"	"Work is fun"

Team functioning

Think about how your team is functioning at this time. Are any internal team issues inhibiting progress? Is conflict being used to create new ideas and focus energy on getting great results? What could your team do differently to avoid becoming stagnant and instead thrive as a Next Level Team?

EXPANDING TEAM PROBLEM SOLVING
AND DECISION MAKING

One of the most powerful and exciting attributes of teams is their ability to solve complex work problems. We have seen many cases where Next Level Teams solved some of their organization's most difficult production or service problems.

Remember, when people are discouraged for any reason, refocusing attention on their strengths can produce amazing results. Collectively, team members have great strength in their ability to resolve problems or innovate and improve work processes. The diverse talents and experience that exist in a team are powerful resources for overcoming organizational and team challenges. Step 2 is an opportune time for your team to search for areas of improvement and problem solve to meet its primary responsibilities.

Team members can ask the team leader or their management about important issues the team can tackle. Or they might brainstorm issues that are ripe for improvement, discuss each issue, and select the one that could have real impact but would not stretch the team beyond its abilities.

At this point your team should focus energy on finding new and exciting solutions. Be sure to listen to each other, build on

•

differences in team members' ideas, and come to a decision that feels right to all members of the team. Keep talking about the decision until it is accepted by everyone. Following this decision-making process can do wonders for a team's self-confidence. The team will undoubtedly use the experience to decide on new ways to solve problems or take advantage of opportunities.

Don't forget that once the team has completed its project, a celebration is in order. Celebrate the power of team decision making and the results that follow!

◎ **QUESTIONS TO CONSIDER**

A challenge for the team

Think about your team's work responsibilities (team goals), and list some opportunities for improvement (for example, improved quality, reduced cost, or enhanced service delivery). Which opportunity would be worth tackling? What will your team have to do to succeed in this challenge? How do you think you and your team members will feel after the improvements are made?

Nothing great is created suddenly, any more than a bunch of grapes or a fig. If you tell me that you desire a fig, I answer you that there must be time. Let it first blossom, then bear fruit, then ripen.

EPICTETUS 50-120

DISCOURAGEMENT AND CHANGE:
THE END OF STEP 2

As we come to the end of our discussion of step 2, we hope you are feeling that you have some ideas to help counter the negative forces of the valley of discouragement. Indeed, if you use the ideas in this and the previous two chapters, your team can accelerate the movement to the Next Level. It is critical that teams remain focused on the long-term, big picture of what their work and work life will be like under the new system. Use information sharing to keep building trust and empowering people to act responsibly. Use wider boundaries and expanded team decision making to prove to the team that it can make a difference and become a Next Level Team.

 EXAMPLES

The pharmaceutical team moves ahead

Members of a three-year-old team at a prominent pharmaceutical company commented to us that at the outset, they were fearful and frustrated by their new responsibilities. It seemed to them that they were taking on responsibilities beyond their abilities, and they doubted they could learn the new skills required.

However, by using the ideas in these last three chapters to help develop the skills of a Next Level Team, they have become a highly developed team, completely confident in their abilities to perform the needed tasks. All team members commented that they have benefited personally through this role expansion and that work is more interesting and enjoyable. They also said that they would never want to return to the previous system. Having worked their way through the valley of discouragement, they have emerged stronger, both individually and collectively.

•

AS WE TRANSITION TO STEP 3

As you and your team members take on more ownership of your work and related issues, and as you learn to use the skills of information sharing, boundary clarification, and self-managing teams, you are coming to the end of step 2. You are moving out of the valley of discouragement by

- Making use of the skills people already possess
- Acquiring new skills needed at the Next Level
- Enhancing team processes
- Expanding team decision making and problem solving

As you reach full acceleration onto the superhighway to the Next Level, you are ready to move to step 3, where we will focus on how you and your team can master the skills of Next Level Teams.

•

Freedom is the opportunity to make decisions.

KENNETH HILDEBRAND

Make Team Decisions to Create a Sense of Power

Master
the Skills

EIGHT

Use Information to Drive Great Results

When teams get through step 2, the joy of acceleration often becomes a problem for making the final step to the Next Level. It is tempting for people to take their eyes off the vision of a fully functioning Next Level Team. As we have learned, these teams focus not only on more involvement for team members but also on expanded responsibility for achieving great results. Next Level Teams have important responsibilities for everyone on the team. In Next Level Teams, people voice their opinions, disagree with one another, argue for their positions, and feel the pressure of performance responsibility. People also feel a sense of ownership, are listened to and understood, make and implement team decisions, and make use of and further develop every member's talents.

As you move into this last step of the journey, a number of questions remain:

- We have had some success with these new team skills, but will we be able to fully master the skills so they become new habits?

- Is the effort to master the skills really worth it? Will our leadership let us go all the way and become a true Next Level Team?

- Are we really making a positive impact in terms of the results we are achieving? Are they really great results?

- Who is not yet onboard with the new team approach, and how do we get them more involved?

- Our team is doing better working as a team, but can we work together more effectively and really be a Next Level Team? What is inhibiting us?

- How can we take on an even more significant role in the business? Can we get involved in strategic decisions and other critical issues?

Let's consider how information can be used to help address these questions and move the team closer to its ultimate goal.

HOW CAN BETTER USE OF INFORMATION KEEP THE CHANGE PROCESS GOING?

At this point in the change process, teams are really beginning to use the information that they have received during the first two steps of the change. They have also seen how the information they have begun to share with management is valuable in better managerial decisions. Because of this better utilization of information and the two-way sharing of information, they are now in a better position to know what additional information they need to enhance their performance.

It is time for your team to discuss how it is using the information it now has available about site and organization performance. Could the team use additional information on particular issues? Less information on others? Information in a different format or time frame? Discussing such questions will help senior leadership and your team ensure that they are placing value and importance on the same information and using the same measurements to track success. If inconsistencies exist between the information being used by your team and by senior leadership, the result will be wasted effort. It is critical for the team to be clear on what information is most closely related to the goals of the company. At this stage, it is also imperative for senior leadership to listen to what the team feels is important to measure relative to those goals.

Knowledge desires always increase; it is like fire,

which must first be kindled by some external agent,

but which will afterwards propagate itself.

DR. SAMUEL JOHNSON

★ **EXAMPLES**

Using information in a packaging company

One company in the packaging industry slowly over time gave complete control of business results to the teams in the company. Each team was set up as a little company within the larger company. The teams controlled the information-sharing process, asking for what they needed and generating a great deal of their own information.

Once a quarter, all the teams came together to share their results for the quarter and relate them to the overall company performance. The combined reports of the teams were rolled up into a company profit-and-loss statement for the quarter, along with *other key measurements of performance, such as waste, machine downtime, packages shipped, turnover, and cost per unit of production. Through an open dialogue at these meetings, everyone learned what key measurements were being used to assess company performance and what new ones might be needed to enhance accuracy. The impact on team morale, energy, and involvement was almost as amazing as the impact on company results.*

⊚ **QUESTIONS TO CONSIDER**

Additional information

Now that your team has been in the process of receiving and using new types of information to achieve results, what additional information could help the team operate even more effectively and help it make better business decisions? Also, could any information be modified in timing or format to be more useful?

DETERMINING WHAT INFORMATION IS UNNECESSARY

At this stage of the journey, your team has a great deal of experience with using information and has a much better idea what information is needed to achieve its goals. Your team may decide that some of the information it has been receiving is just not necessary. By identifying what information is not needed, the team can help streamline the information-sharing process. It is important to recognize that information needs may change as problems are solved, goals are achieved, and issues are addressed.

•

Collecting useless data

One of our clients had recently won the coveted Deming quality award. The process of applying for the award had led people in the organization to collect great volumes of data. In fact, they had become so used to collecting data that they were gathering it on almost everything they did. For example, they measured the response time of the receptionists for over a year and found a very steady pattern. Response time dropped off between 11:30 a.m. and 12:30 p.m. and between 1:00 p.m. and 2:00 p.m. They found that response time was slower when one of the two receptionists went on a lunch break and was faster when both were present. Nobody had bothered to ask if that slowing of response time actually created a problem. When the receptionists found it did not create a problem, they stopped collecting this useless data. If, on the other hand, the slower response time had created a problem, they could have identified a measure of the problem and begun to address it.

QUESTIONS TO CONSIDER

Unnecessary information

Is your team now receiving any information that is no longer particularly useful, and could the team stop receiving it with no great loss?

REVISITING INFORMATION SHARING AND TRUST

As more and more information is requested by teams to help them make better decisions, the issue of trust will continually need to be addressed. As teams begin to ask for sensitive information, the leadership may be tempted to limit some types of information. It is critical to the long-term success of the Next

Information sharing is, quite simply, the lifeblood of a Next Level Team. But it needs to be the right information at the right time to get great results.

Level Teams to trust them with whatever information they feel they need. If leaders feel the information is particularly sensitive or could be damaging in the hands of competitors, they need to say that and then trust the teams to guard the information carefully. It is certainly in the teams' best interest to do so, as well as in the interest of management and the company. Remember that sharing sensitive information compliments both the intellect and integrity of team members, and both factors are needed at the Next Level.

 EXAMPLES

Saving the wire harness plant

In 1981 Xerox Corporation announced that for economic reasons it would be subcontracting the assembly of wire harnesses used in its copiers and closing the harness assembly department of about 180 people. Since the company a year earlier had initiated an employee involvement process called "Quality of Worklife," the union was concerned that this unilateral decision, which affected so many lives, contradicted the principles of the process.

Meetings between the union and management led to a temporary suspension of the decision until a study team could look at the issue. The team—composed of six workers from the affected area, an engineer, and a manager—were given six months to find ways to improve quality, cost, and delivery performance of the business to levels that would assure a positive competitive position and, ultimately, secure jobs.

•

The team was given specific information about the department's work. In particular, the team learned that it would need to identify approximately $3.2 million in savings to be competitive with subcontractors.

In 1981 it was unusual for companies to place such responsibility in a team of workers. But the teams at Xerox were valued as important contributors to the success of the company. The study team received the sensitive and critical information it needed to perform an analysis of the issues. The proposals the team presented covered a broad range of options that significantly exceeded the team's target of $3.2 million. The decision to subcontract the wire harness work was canceled and the 180 jobs at Xerox were saved. These results would not have been possible without management trusting the team, providing it with sensitive information, and involving it in a critical decision.

⊚ **QUESTIONS TO CONSIDER**

Protecting sensitive information

Think about the issue of trust as it relates to management sharing sensitive information with your team. How can your team ensure that such information will be carefully controlled and used in the most effective manner?

HELPING NEW TEAM MEMBERS

In today's dynamic society, it is important to acknowledge that the membership of a Next Level Team will change from time to time. People will leave the team and new members will take their place. If they come from inside the company, they may be familiar with Next Level Teams, but someone coming from the outside may not. In either case, you must recognize that your team will have its own unique vision, mission, values, methods, and processes. Both outsiders and insiders will need information about your team if they are to become productive and be assimilated by your team without becoming a drag on the Next Level processes you have developed.

Ideally, your team will possess a clear statement that summarizes its work, its methods, and its beliefs. This statement should also include the organization's vision, mission, and values and how the team's purpose and goals align with them. New team members will also need to understand the team's norms and ground rules for working together, as well as the individual task roles for each member of the team.

Communication strategies, both inside the team and with other teams, also need to be spelled out for new members. Additionally, new members need to learn about any specific internal team processes, such as those for problem solving, decision making, conflict resolution, team meetings, and more. In short, new team members, whether insiders or outsiders, need a crash course in your Next Level Team so they can be fully functioning members and not detriments.

 QUESTIONS TO CONSIDER

Orienting a new team member

Think about the challenge of teaching new team members. How can you help new team members learn about your team's tasks, methods, norms, and beliefs in the shortest time possible?

MASTERING INFORMATION SHARING
FOR THE NEXT LEVEL

As you move into step 3 of the change to Next Level Teams, you must come to a new understanding of the role and use of information. You must make the break from the traditional use of information by managers and employees.

Most of us were reared in a system that clearly defined who possessed various types of information. Managers had access to certain kinds of sensitive information that employees could not see. We must change that old habit. Today there is incredible public access to information. People are better informed now than at any time in history. Organizations that continue to restrict access to information invite uninformed decision making and low levels of trust. Only by allowing team members to have access to most of the information management has can an organization expect to gain the benefits of the Next Level—teams that use their knowledge, experience, and motivation to achieve outstanding results.

Information sharing for Next Level Teams is a two-way street. Team members have lots of information that managers do not possess, and they cannot persist in playing the game of withholding information just because management does not require them to share it. Next Level Team members are full-fledged team members who share responsibility and commitment for achieving great results. They must make good use of information that is provided to them and at the same time provide information that can be useful to management. In addition, team members need to make their needs known to leaders and demonstrate how access to new and sensitive information will benefit the team and its contribution to the overall system.

•

As we conclude our discussion of mastering the skill of information sharing, remember two important facts:

- The skill of information sharing must be mastered by all parties to be most effective for a Next Level Team.
- With a greater flow and use of information, the team is ready to expand boundaries so wide that it replaces them with vision and values.

•

The kind of thinking that led to past success will not lead to future success.

KEN BLANCHARD, ALAN RANDOLPH,
AND JOHN CARLOS

NINE

Replace Boundaries with Vision and Values

Now that your team has the information to drive results, your journey to becoming a successful Next Level Team needs to focus on shifting the boundaries of behavior so they come from within the team members. The intent is to incorporate boundaries into the belief systems of team members so they can exercise good judgment and make decisions that support and uphold the organization's vision, mission, and values.

This is not to imply that direction and boundaries are not needed from the leadership. It is to suggest that the broad boundaries that guide team member behavior need to be moved as much as possible into the hearts and minds of the team members. *Full Steam Ahead! Unleash the Power of Vision in Your Company and Your Life* by Ken Blanchard and Jesse Stoner provides an excellent framework for organizing your vision, mission, and values.

MAKING THE "RIGHT" DECISION

The decisions that we make each day in our personal and professional lives are determined by those values and beliefs that we have acquired since birth, plus additional operating values that we have learned in our organizations. These values help us determine what we believe to be right or wrong, good or bad, and normal or not normal. These values are a key factor in any decision-making process.

While personal and organizational values provide a moral and ethical foundation for decision making, the vision provides direction. When team members can see the vision and understand the basic operating values of their organization, decision making becomes far easier and more productive. For example,

- When faced with a decision that requires us to choose between satisfying a customer or upholding a company policy, what should we do?

- If maintaining a production schedule means sacrificing quality, should we do it?

- If a call from a customer exceeds the organization's guideline of two minutes, should we hang up or continue our efforts to meet the customer's need?

- If we see a way to improve our team's effectiveness, do we take time away from production to work on it?

These are just a few of the many questions that face team members each day. Since it is impossible for leadership to deal with such a volume of situations, team members can greatly enhance organizational effectiveness and efficiency if they are able to act on their own to resolve questions such as these. In fact, this is perhaps the greatest benefit of moving to Next Level Teams—the ability of team members to deal with complex day-to-day issues in a responsible and timely manner.

The key, however, is making sure that team members understand the direction and beliefs or vision and values of the organization so that responsible, informed decisions can be made.

WIDENING BOUNDARIES TO
ENHANCE TEAM CONTRIBUTION

A great visual analogy that we use in our work with companies is to have people think of the sidelines of a football field and then ask them, "Who has the widest playing field (boundaries) in the company?" In a hierarchy it is clearly the CEO, and each level of management down the hierarchy has a smaller playing field. By the time you get to the frontline people, the playing field can be very narrow indeed.

In a Next Level Team environment, these boundaries are gradually widened as people learn to act with responsibility and use their skills to get the work done. By this final step along the journey, the boundaries may still not be as wide as those for the CEO, but they are far wider than they were when the process began. The boundaries provide guidelines for the autonomy of all members of the organization, and they also build responsibility and values into every person in the company.

Knowledge once gained casts a light beyond

its own immediate boundaries.

JOHN TYNDALL

Confusion over organizational values

During a management training session with a health maintenance organization (HMO), the subject of values and beliefs was being discussed. Wanting to test his management team, the CEO posed a dilemma from an actual recent situation. Their company had been asked to pay for a lifesaving operation needed by one of their policyholders. Without the operation, the person would die. However, the policy excluded this operation from the person's coverage.

The management team broke into small groups to discuss the dilemma. When they returned and began to discuss the situation, they offered different opinions on how to handle it. Some felt that helping the patient get the needed care was the morally correct thing to do, while others felt the company could not remain in business if it paid such claims. The CEO was astonished and dismayed. He truly felt that every manager would know that the company would never let any of its policyholders die in such a circumstance. However, he learned a powerful lesson with respect to communicating and clarifying the organization's values to his people.

In complex decision-making situations it is essential for people to understand the purpose of the organization, its core values, and its beliefs.

VISION, MISSION, AND VALUES
AS BOUNDARIES FOR YOUR TEAM

How do your organization's vision, mission, and values affect behavior and decisions at work? For these guideposts to be meaningful and useful, they must be translated into daily behaviors and actions.

Your vision, mission, and values

Think about your organization's vision, mission, and values. Can you state them? Are they clear? Can you translate them into your own words?

EXAMPLES

Helping customers versus selling products

The CEO of a Delaware high-tech electronics research and manufacturing organization had a strong belief in customer service. He believed that the company's role in a blossoming technology industry was to help its customers solve problems.

One day he posed a hypothetical question to his people: "If a customer had a problem that could be solved better by one of our competitor's products, would you recommend it?" His answer, in line with his values, was an unequivocal yes.

He believed that by truly helping the customer solve a problem, he was not only doing the right thing, but also showing the customer that his organization was a trusted resource. By creating a dialogue around his question and answer, he helped his people understand that their role was to help customers solve problems, not just sell products. The dialogue left no doubt about how he wanted them to respond in such a situation.

•

EXPAND YOUR TEAM'S ROLE EVEN FURTHER

At the beginning of the Next Level Team development process, you and your team members were asked to take responsibility for more decisions that affected your work. These decisions may have included things such as maintaining safety and housekeeping, measuring customer service and quality, and selecting work methods.

As the journey progressed, you probably began to take on more complex decisions, such as determining training needs, repairing equipment, providing cross-training, and scheduling production.

At this point, the role that you and your team members play must once again be expanded to reflect your growth and maturity as a Next Level Team. In the domain of decision making, mature teams are challenged to take on an expanded scope and complexity of decisions. For example, your team will need to decide when and how to engage in cross-functional teaming (collaborating with other teams), whom to hire for new positions, and how to prepare budgets.

 EXAMPLES

The maintenance team takes on more responsibility

The maintenance team of a four-hundred-person pump manufacturing company had been moving steadily for two years toward operating as a highly functioning Next Level Team. The team's manager had gradually given the members more authority for the operation of their team, and they had accepted the responsibility well.

•

As their company's work grew and shifts were expanded, it became obvious that the team would need to add another mechanic. After discussing this issue, the manager and team members agreed that the team should conduct the hiring process. The members had already developed standards for each position within the team and had even developed their own performance appraisal system with the help of the human resources (HR) department. They were well prepared to understand the skills and abilities they needed from the new mechanic.

After learning the do's and don'ts of interviewing potential employees, the team members interviewed, selected, and hired their new team member. However, after the three-month trial period it was obvious that the new-hire had exaggerated her abilities and was unable to perform some of the skills desperately needed by the team. The team members discussed their situation and decided termination was in order. At that point they thought about turning over the termination process to the manager. However, they came to the conclusion that since they had hired the new mechanic, it was up to them to terminate her employment.

Once again working through the HR department, just as any good manager would in this situation, they conducted the termination in a fair and caring manner. Throughout the process every team member felt the pain associated with the decision, but it left all of them stronger and more dedicated to improving how they would seek out and hire new candidates.

A team should never practice on a field that is not lined. Your players have to become aware of the field's boundaries.

JOHN MADDEN

•
Replace Boundaries with Vision and Values

Assuming total responsibility

Think about the roles that your team has taken on during its development as a highly functioning Next Level Team. What remaining roles and decisions would be appropriate to add if your team is to assume total responsibility for its operation?

TEAMS AS BUSINESS PARTNERS

At this point in the journey to Next Level Teams, your team must now begin to work as a real business partner with management. Frontline team members, team leaders, and senior leaders must begin to act like true equals in terms of accepting responsibility for the success of the organization. Each person will have a different role, but everyone will share responsibility for organizational success.

Positive and negative feedback on performance can flow up, down, and sideways in the organization. Frontline team members should provide ideas to senior leadership and expect action, just as senior leadership should expect a response from frontline team members. Information sharing flows in all directions, with origination and response coming from whichever source is most appropriate.

For example, frontline workers are closer to the action of production or service delivery. They may observe events or collect data that are unavailable to senior leadership. As partners, it is their job to interpret and share that information with team leaders, members of other teams, and senior leadership.

Senior leadership, on the other hand, may have more knowledge about industry trends and global events that impact the business. It is the leaders' job to share this information with the teams and help them understand its significance.

All parties have a responsibility to act on information as appropriate, making decisions to fix or improve conditions and inform others of what they are planning to do. Business partners work together for the good of the organization, and partner actions must be encouraged and expected by all parties at this stage of the journey. Having wider boundaries will help keep everyone working for the same end results.

◎ **QUESTIONS TO CONSIDER**

Acting like a business partner

Think about what it means for your team to work like a business partner with your organization's leadership. What does your team already do that directly impacts the organization's vision, mission, and results? What additional responsibilities could you take on to become a more significant business partner?

USING VISION AND VALUES FOR TEAM SUCCESS

For any organization to expect its people to operate in a highly effective manner, the decisions made by team members must be driven by internal beliefs that reflect the organization's purpose and direction. These internal beliefs provide a self-correcting monitor for the behavior of people. But for this mechanism to work correctly, the organization's vision and values must be crystal clear. Otherwise, people will be moving in different—sometimes even opposing—directions that usually hurt performance.

Leaders must take the time to communicate and model the vision and values desired for the organization. Team members must inquire into, discuss, and internalize the vision and values so they can make business decisions that move the organization toward that vision using behaviors that are consistent with the values of the organization.

The result of this use of vision and values is an organization whose members function as partners who are in agreement with its purpose, operating values, and hopes for the future. From such agreement comes a powerful mechanism for the highly effective functioning of Next Level Teams.

•

Simply pushing harder within the old boundaries will not do.

KARL WEICK

TEN

Be a Next Level Team and Get Great Results

At this stage of the journey your team possesses information that used to be almost exclusively in the hands of management. Team members also have a clear vision and a set of operating values. By combining information with clear boundaries and team skills, your team can now draw on its collective knowledge, experience, and motivation to achieve impressive results.

More specifically, you and your team members can now make many of the decisions that your supervisor or management previously made. For example, you can handle new team member interviewing and hiring, conduct team member performance evaluations, handle individual performance problems, prepare and monitor budgets, and arrange for equipment purchases. With information and clear boundaries, your team can identify problems or potential problems and initiate plans for resolving them before they become severe.

What you need now is to continually encourage one another as team members so that you can actually reach the Next Level. As a Next Level Team, you will have achieved total team competence. Your team members will feel confident about fully using everyone's collective talents to achieve great results.

·

Clarifying expectations

A company in the pollution control design field initially found it difficult to make the shift to full responsibility. The team members vividly recalled their frustration and dissatisfaction as they were learning new skills and did not like the idea of having to deal with performance problems of team members.

Their solution was to make sure that everyone had a clear understanding of the team's direction and that their expectations of each other were completely understood. As a result, they found that performance problems occurred less frequently than in the past, and the problems were easier to resolve because they were spotted much earlier. Clear communication about direction and expectations allowed everyone to function as a team that worked well together to achieve great results.

QUESTIONS TO CONSIDER

The skills of a next level team

Think about what you've learned as your team has moved through this book and toward the Next Level. What are the new skills you have acquired that help you work well as a team?

HOW TO MAINTAIN A HIGH PERFORMANCE NEXT LEVEL TEAM

Once your team has developed into an energized, high performance work team, an important task will be to keep it there. Without constant vigilance, the team may find itself falling back into old behaviors. Anything we do repeatedly sometimes becomes tedious, maybe even boring. So a challenge for the team is to keep it fresh.

MEASURE WORK PERFORMANCE

Doing the work is one thing; improving it is quite another. What determines success in our work? What determines good performance? The only real way to find out is to measure it.

Just about anything can be measured: goods produced per minute or hour or day, letters written per day, sales volume, calls made to prospective customers, downtime, scrap and waste, cycle time (for example, time from the initial customer order to shipping), changeover time (time to prepare for a different product run), and more. The list of activities involved in work is almost endless, providing a host of opportunities for measurement and improvement.

Next Level Teams excel because they are always finding improved ways of working together to produce great results.

⭐ **EXAMPLES**

Creating useful measures

The maintenance team at a manufacturing plant had been working its way toward Next Level status when team members realized that they had no way of knowing how they were doing. How, *they wondered,* can you measure maintenance and repair work when it is mostly the one-of-a-kind variety?

The team decided to survey the members of the workforce about what they really wanted and needed in a good maintenance team. They began by surveying the supervisors who usually called them for maintenance work. What they heard from the plant supervisors was

•

- *We want you to respond to our need quickly (later defined as fifteen minutes).*

- *We want you to complete the work within a reasonable time period (later defined as eight hours).*

- *We don't want to have to call you back later for the same work (in other words, the quality of the work should be so high that you will not have to redo it).*

Having defined the criteria for a good maintenance team, they set out to create a way to measure their performance. They developed a form that would capture the information. Then they found a way to chart the results weekly. Initially, they found that they were able to meet these criteria about 80 percent of the time. They began working on ideas to improve their ability to meet the criteria and within a year were successful 97 percent of the time.

One of their ideas for improvement dealt with the first criterion, responding to maintenance calls within fifteen minutes. The maintenance shop was a noisy area and sometimes they could not hear the phone ringing. So they connected a bright light to the phone that was activated whenever it rang. Through this innovation, they were able to eliminate missed calls.

These great results were brought about by defining and measuring the team's high performance criteria as defined by their customers.

MEASURE HOW THE TEAM IS FUNCTIONING

You can not only keep your team from deteriorating, but you can, in fact, keep it growing in various ways. One way is for the team to periodically measure how it is functioning as a team. In addition to normal performance measurements that the team uses daily to measure progress against its goals, at least quarterly the team should conduct a team process evaluation. This can be accomplished in several ways, but one of the best is to use a team assessment tool that measures overall team performance. Each team member completes a questionnaire and scores it. Then team members meet to discuss results. These evaluations help expose and pinpoint specific team problems, allowing your team to resolve them before they become flash points.

 EXAMPLES

The sales team assesses itself

Once we were asked to help two sales teams in a fish-importing business. These teams sold fish to restaurants, groceries, and retail fish markets. The work was intense, as each salesperson was constantly on the phone with customers, attempting to meet daily and monthly goals.

Financially, the teams were successful, and team members generally were motivated by the excitement of their work. As part of our assessment we used a tool called the "Team Effectiveness Profile," which highlighted what team members thought about their performance.[3] The overall result showed one team to be "immature," which was the lowest of five possible rankings. This ranking was associated with a team that had not begun to develop task and process skills and was very dependent on its appointed leader for direction, decisions, and support. The profile also showed that the team was weakest in the category of "group interpersonal relationships."

When team members met to discuss the results, they talked about how their work and its demanding goals left little time for supporting each other and developing satisfying, productive relationships. Each one said that this was the greatest source of discontent with his or her job.

For the first time, every team member was able to see that each one of them was dissatisfied with the current situation and wanted to change it. With this new information the team members found ways to provide each other more support and build their relationships, and a subsequent survey confirmed that they had made good progress.

EVALUATE DAILY

A simple method for maintaining and improving team performance is to evaluate smaller functions. For example, meetings are notorious for not accomplishing what is intended. To ensure productivity, all team meetings should end with a verbal evaluation by team members. In this evaluation—which usually lasts less than five minutes—each team member states what went well in the meeting and what could be improved. When evaluations are performed repeatedly, team members begin to hone their meeting management skills.

BUILD THE TEAM USING OFF-SITE EXPERIENCES

Another method of keeping your team growing and alive is to take members off-site periodically for a "battery charge." Whole Foods Market, Inc., a chain of health-oriented grocery stores with an effective team process, directs all of its teams to schedule and hold annual off-site team-building sessions. This means, for example, that the Produce Team at Store X must schedule and design its own team-building session once a year. This demonstrates the company's commitment to team and team member development.

At these sessions, team members learn about team communication, listening skills, conflict resolution, personality differences, personal values, store financial accounting, budgeting, gain-sharing strategies, process improvement, and more.

RECOGNITION

Another way of maintaining energy and team unity is for members to periodically recognize each other for something noteworthy. Recognition is simply a thank-you paid to another member for a valued contribution. This is also a good opportunity to enlist the involvement of your team's leadership.

Building and maintaining team spirit is vitally important to the long-term health and vitality of your team and its members. Often lackluster performance and behavior in organizations stems from a lack of awareness of the human needs of people at work. People need to be recognized for their good work, and organizations, departments, and teams that pay attention to these needs tend to outperform others by a wide margin.

◎ **QUESTIONS TO CONSIDER**

Measurement

As you think about your work, what do you measure now? What are the key performance indicators that would really tell you how you're doing? What should you start measuring regularly that you do not now measure?

RAISE THE BAR: LOOK FOR NEW OPPORTUNITIES

Your team should continue to raise the bar of performance standards to stay ahead of competitors in other companies. Your team must join senior leadership in looking outside the organization for information about what competitors are doing and what customers need and want, as well as for new ideas that range well beyond the industry in which the company operates.

EXAMPLES

Teams analyze competitors

In the food processing industry, one company's teams began analyzing competitors to generate new ideas for their own development. When teams began presenting information about their competitors' productivity rates, new machinery, profit-and-loss statements, and other "sensitive" information, company leaders were alarmed. They were truly concerned that their teams had overzealously crossed the border of industrial espionage.

When they inquired about how the teams acquired their information, the teams responded that every bit of information was obtained through public sources. Information about new production lines and productivity was obtained from articles in industry journals, and profit-and-loss information was obtained through stockholder annual reports. One of the teams had purchased a share of stock in each of the competitor companies so that it could obtain this financial information regularly.

When the senior leaders heard this they were relieved, and they were also impressed by the ingenuity of their teams.

The secretary develops a new business

A medium-sized food processing and sales company listened to a secretary's idea for developing a new market for the company's products. Prior to her suggestion, the company had sold only to wholesalers, who in turn sold to grocery stores. The secretary suggested starting a catalogue business to provide a direct avenue to customers. She was encouraged to pursue the idea, and after one year the catalogue business she was running had grown to over a million dollars in sales, with the promise of growing far more.

Ingenuity knows no bounds.

UNKNOWN

BEING A NEXT LEVEL TEAM WITH A FUTURE

Throughout this book, we have worked to help your team clarify where it is going and how it is going to get there. We have covered a number of topics relevant to team development designed to help your work group become a highly effective Next Level Team.

Your team is moving forward during one of the most significant transition periods of the postindustrial business age. Regardless of any bumps in the road you may encounter, understand that you are breaking new ground in how organizations work. You and your leaders are to be commended for your foresight and persistence in moving your organization to a new level of functioning and, ultimately, a new level of performance. Your team is now in a position to contribute to the business in extraordinary ways.

Your team is also in a position to generate self-development opportunities so that growth becomes a way of life. This is the time to broaden your horizons and think about new areas that would add value to your team's work and its operation. Look into the future and see what new challenges and opportunities await your team.

 QUESTIONS TO CONSIDER

Prepare for a great future

Your team is now a Next Level Team. What can you do now to prepare for your team's future and make use of these new skills that you have mastered?

•

*When a team outgrows individual performance
and learns team confidence, excellence becomes a reality.*

JOE PATERNO

ELEVEN

Congratulations

your team has made it to the Next Level

What a journey this has been. When you began this book, you did not even know what a Next Level Team was, much less how to become one. You most likely have had some good experiences in team settings but also some bad ones. Now you can appreciate what we mean when we say that Next Level Teams

- Use all team members' ideas and motivation
- Make better use of the team members' and team leader's time
- Increase productivity and satisfaction for you, your team, and the organization

Take a moment and give yourself credit for knowing more now than when you started reading this book. You know what to expect from a Next Level Team and how good it can feel to be a part of such a fantastic team of people.

But you know a lot more than just what to expect. You know how to use the skills that make a team a Next Level Team. By working through the three steps outlined in this book, you

1. Took on the challenge to begin learning Next Level skills

2. Accelerated the change—just when you had developed doubts

3. Mastered the three critical skills of a Next Level Team

Your persistence has paid off big time because *you* and *your team are better off now than you were before.* So give yourself and your teammates a big pat on the back for sticking to the process and seeing it through.

Because you chose to stay the course, you and your team know how to function as a Next Level Team. You know how to use the three skills that put your team way above the average work group. You have learned to

- Use information sharing that flows up, down, and sideways to build high levels of trust and responsibility for your team

- Use clear boundaries that are now quite wide to create freedom for your team to act with responsibility and clear focus

- Use self-managing skills to make effective team decisions on complex issues and to get great results for your team and organization

TIME TO CELEBRATE

Now take some time with your team to celebrate your achievement of becoming a Next Level Team. All of you are to be applauded for learning to use and apply these critical skills. Knowledge is a wonderful thing in the hands of a team of people who are willing to use that knowledge to get great results! We know you will enjoy the challenge of being at the Next Level and the pride that comes with achieving exceptional results.

Congratulations on becoming a Next Level Team!

·

•

NOTES

1. Larry Armstrong and Geoff Smith, "Productivity Assured—or We'll Fix Them Free," *BusinessWeek*, November 25, 1991.
2. W. Alan Randolph and Barry Z. Posner *Checkered Flag Projects: 10 Rules for Creating and Managing Projects That Win!* (Upper Saddle River, NJ: Prentice Hall PTR, 2002), 12–15.
3. Rollin Glaser and Christine Glaser, Copyright 1980–2003 Organization Design and Development, Inc., available at Teambuildinginc.com.

INDEX

•

KEN BLANCHARD and **ALAN RANDOLPH** (alanran@comcast.net) work with organizations the world over through the Ken Blanchard Companies, which is committed to helping people and organizations lead at a higher level. With a mission to unleash the power and potential of people and organizations for the greater good, the company is a global leader in workplace learning, productivity, and leadership effectiveness. The Ken Blanchard Companies believes that people are the key to accomplishing strategic objectives. Its programs not only help people learn but also ensure that they cross the bridge from learning to doing. The company offers seminars and provides in-depth consulting in the areas of teamwork, customer service, leadership, performance management, and organizational synergy. To learn more, visit the Web site at www.kenblanchard .com or browse the eStore at www.kenblanchard.com/estore.

The Ken Blanchard Companies
125 State Place, Escondido, CA 92029
800-728-6000 or 760-489-5005   Fax: 760-489-8407

PETER GRAZIER has his own company (www.teambuildinginc .com) that focuses on developing stronger teams in organizations. Please contact him at

Teambuilding, Inc.
1 Pine Lane, Chadds Ford, PA 19317
610-358-1961
e-mail: Inquire@teambuilding.com

LINKING *GO TEAM!* TO IMPORTANT
TEAM CONCEPTS FROM PREVIOUS BOOKS

Both the foreword and introduction to this book noted the vital need for people to work effectively in teams to succeed in today's global and dynamic business environment. We also made the point that this focus on teams has been growing for several decades. *Go Team!* did not just appear out of nowhere. It is grounded in the concepts of previous books on teams, and it expands those concepts to focus more fully on tapping the talents and motivation of people to achieve great results.

The main foundation upon which *Go Team!* is based is the book titled *The One Minute Manager Builds High Performing Teams.* This classic and very popular book focuses on the characteristics of high performing teams, as well as the stages of team development and the leadership behaviors that facilitate team development. The characteristics of a High Performing Team are summarized in the PERFORM acronym, which appears in the diagram that follows.

The popular sequel, *High Five! The Magic of Working Together,* uses a story about a father working with his son's hockey team to focus on process outcomes for high performing teams. These key ingredients for a winning team are summarized in the acronym PUCK, which also appears in the diagram that follows.

What we have done in *Go Team! Take Your Team to the Next Level* is to focus on team members owning the responsibility for making important decisions and achieving great results. And to take ownership for decisions and results, team members must learn to release and focus their knowledge, experience, and motivation by using three important skills:

- Use *information sharing* to build high levels of trust and responsibility.

- Use *clear boundaries* to create the freedom to act responsibly.

- Use *self-managing skills* to make decisions and get great results.

These three Next Level skills also appear in the diagram that follows.

As you have read this book, you have learned to use the three Next Level skills. From the diagram on the next page, you can see how the three ownership skills from *Go Team!* build upon the behavioral characteristics of the PERFORM model and are integrated with the key ingredients of winning teams developed in *High Five!*

The outcome is that you and your team are now ready to achieve great results for yourselves and your organization. *Go Team!*

The One Minute Manager Builds High Performing Teams 1990, 2000	High Five! The Magic of Working Together 2001	Go Team! Take Your Team to the Next Level 2005
Behavioral Characteristics	*Key Ingredients of Winning Teams*	*Creating Ownership*

Purpose and Values

Providing Purpose and Values

Empowerment

Clear Boundaries of Freedom and Responsibility

Relationships and Communication

Unleashing and Developing Skills

Self-Managing Skills

Flexibility

Creating Team Power

Information Sharing to Build Trust and Responsibility

Optimal Performance

Keeping the Accent on the Positive

Recognition and Appreciation

Morale

TOGETHER PRODUCE

GREAT RESULTS FOR TEAM MEMBERS, LEADERS, AND THE ORGANIZATION

·

TEAM PRAISINGS

Books like ours do not just appear out of nowhere. Over numerous years, ideas germinate and eventually result in a concept for a book. Then it takes a great deal of encouragement to move from concept to final product. Along the way to completion of this book you hold in your hands, many people have influenced and supported our efforts. We cannot possibly thank everyone who has had an impact on our thinking about teams, but here are a few very special people who come to mind. For others we do not mention, please forgive us and know that you are appreciated nonetheless.

Steve Piersanti, with Berrett-Koehler Publishers, deserves a whopping big praising for pushing and pushing us to make this book better and better. He helped bring us down to earth on many an occasion yet was always kind and supportive and focused on creating a book that would be useful to those who chose to read and share it.

Also at Berrett-Koehler, we owe a big praising to Jeevan Sivasubramaniam, better known as Jeevan S., for keeping up with all the details and deadlines that kept us moving forward

·

toward a finished product. He even helped keep Steve Piersanti on track at times.

Teammates at a variety of companies have been our colleagues and have taught us a great deal about effective teamwork.

Mark Robbins, Jennifer Stanford, and David Heckman, at Robbins-Gioia, Inc., have worked with Alan to create a stronger organization and set of teams in their company, which consults and serves many other companies.

Carmela Southers and Pamela Wagoner, with the Ken Blanchard Companies and Host Marriott, respectively, have taught Alan a lot about working as a team to effect a vision and set of objectives in a large organization.

Susan Steele and John Robison, formerly with HCIA Inc., worked as training and design colleagues with Alan over several years to implement positive organizational change in a growing health services company.

Stephen Sebastian, Virginia Pimentel, and Jose Carabajal, with Cargill, taught Alan about working in a virtual team effort to design a multinational program to teach coaching skills.

Karl Hamlin, an independent IT consultant, taught Alan the value of trust in a team relationship.

Pat West and Kevin Duffy, with PriceWaterhouseCoopers LLP, worked with Alan to create dynamic Web-based classes on project management and helped Alan understand how to work in a virtual team atmosphere.

Numerous colleagues with the Ken Blanchard Companies have been friends, colleagues, and mentors for many years, including but not limited to Pat Zigarmi, Drea Zigarmi, Fred Finch, Laurie Hawkins, Susan Fowler, Dick Ruhe, Dev Ogle, Garry Demarest, Jesse Stoner, Kathleen Martin, and Vicki Halsey.

Don Carew and Eunice Parisi-Carew provided their kind and supportive foreword and, more importantly, their over thirty years of mentoring about teams and friendship.

We have many colleagues with whom a relationship dates back to the early 1970s at the University of Massachusetts, where Ken and Alan first met and where the seeds for this book were born, including, among others, Tony Butterfield, Barry Posner, Gary Powell, Susan Carter, and Joe Litterer (now deceased).

A team of valued colleagues at the Ken Blanchard Companies worked with us to bring this book to publication, including Martha Lawrence and Humberto Medina.

And we must also add a huge praising to our colleague and teammate John Carlos, who wrote two previous books with Ken and Alan and would have been involved in this project had he not suddenly passed away this past year. John was a fantastic storyteller, a wonderful teammate, and an even better friend. We have dedicated this book to his memory. John, you are missed.

Finally, no man in his right mind would ever overlook the support and encouragement from his spouse. We are honored to praise our wives for their unending support and love. Much praise to Margie Blanchard, Ruth Anne Randolph, and Barbara Grazier.

ABOUT THE AUTHORS

KEN BLANCHARD

Few people have made a more positive and lasting impact on the day-to-day management of people and companies than Ken Blanchard. He is the author of several best-selling books, including the blockbuster international best seller *The One Minute Manager* and the giant business bestsellers *Leadership and the One Minute Manager, Raving Fans,* and *Gung Ho!* His books have combined sales of more than eighteen million copies in more than twenty-five languages.

Ken is the chief spiritual officer of the Ken Blanchard Companies, a worldwide human resource development company. He is also cofounder of the Lead Like Jesus Ministries, a non-profit organization dedicated to inspiring and equipping people to be servant leaders in the marketplace. Ken and his wife, Margie, live in San Diego and work with their son, Scott; daughter, Debbie; and Debbie's husband, Humberto Medina.

ALAN RANDOLPH

Alan Randolph is an internationally respected and highly accomplished management educator and consultant. He consults on leadership, teamwork, empowerment, and project management issues for both domestic and international organizations in the public and private sectors. As a consultant, Alan is practical and works effectively with all levels of management, and as a seminar leader, he is relaxed, clear, and to the point.

Alan is a professor of management and international business at the Merrick School of Business, University of Baltimore, and a senior consulting partner with the Ken Blanchard Companies. He has developed a variety of leadership and empowerment products and has published numerous articles in practitioner and academic journals such as *Harvard Business Review, Sloan Management Review, The Academy of Management Executive, Organizational Dynamics,* and *The Academy of Management Journal.*

Alan has also written and coauthored a number of books. His most recent books include *Checkered Flag Projects: 10 Rules for Creating and Managing Projects That Win!* (2002, with Barry Z. Posner), *Empowerment Takes More Than a Minute* (2001, with Ken Blanchard and John P. Carlos), and *The 3 Keys to Empowerment: Release the Power within People for Astonishing Results* (1999, with Ken Blanchard and John P. Carlos).

PETER GRAZIER

After spending years in the construction industry as a civil engineer, Peter Grazier began using employee involvement concepts in 1981 to improve productivity on construction work sites. Having been significantly affected by the results of involving employees directly in work improvement, he formed Teambuilding, Inc., in 1985. Since that time, he has worked with over one hundred organizations in all industries throughout North America and Europe, and his work has been noted in more than eighty publications, including *The Wall Street Journal* and AFL-CIO publications.

•

Peter is the author and publisher of a best-selling book on employee involvement and teamwork. In 1994, he was honored with the prestigious President's Award from the Association for Quality and Participation for his contributions to the field. In January 2000, his Web site, Teambuildinginc.com, was listed by *Harvard Management Update* as one of the "Top 3 Websites for Managers on Teams."

His work encompasses the entire field of organizational collaboration, specifically, employee involvement and empowerment, self-directed work teams, labor-management relations, creativity and innovation, human potential, relationship building, team building, vision-mission-values development, retreat facilitation, and motivational speaking. His training style is entertaining with heavy doses of experiential participant involvement.

common quest is changing the underlying beliefs, mindsets, institutions, and structures that keep generating the same cycles of problems, no matter who our leaders are or what improvement programs we adopt.

We strive to practice what we preach—to operate our publishing company in line with the ideas in our books. At the core of our approach is *stewardship*, which we define as a deep sense of responsibility to administer the company for the benefit of all of our "stakeholder" groups: authors, customers, employees, investors, service providers, and the communities and environment around us. We seek to establish a partnering relationship with each stakeholder that is open, equitable, and collaborative.

We are gratified that thousands of readers, authors, and other friends of the company consider themselves to be part of the "BK Community." We hope that you, too, will join our community and connect with us through the ways described on our website at www.bkconnection.com.

BE CONNECTED

Visit Our Website

Go to www.bkconnection.com to read exclusive previews and excerpts of new books, find detailed information on all Berrett-Koehler titles and authors, browse subject-area libraries of books, and get special discounts.

Subscribe to Our Free E-Newsletter

Be the first to hear about new publications, special discount offers, exclusive articles, news about bestsellers, and more! Get on the list for our free e-newsletter by going to www.bkconnection.com.

Participate in the Discussion

To see what others are saying about our books and post your own thoughts, check out our blogs at www.bkblogs.com.

Get Quantity Discounts

Berrett-Koehler books are available at quantity discounts for orders of ten or more copies. Please call us toll-free at (800) 929-2929 or email us at bkp.orders@aidcvt.com.

Host a Reading Group

For tips on how to form and carry on a book reading group in your workplace or community, see our website at www.bkconnection.com.

Join the BK Community

Thousands of readers of our books have become part of the "BK Community" by participating in events featuring our authors, reviewing draft manuscripts of forthcoming books, spreading the word about their favorite books, and supporting our publishing program in other ways. If you would like to join the BK Community, please contact us at bkcommunity@bkpub.com.